The Fight of Faith Crowned

The Remaining Sermons of Thomas Watson,
Rector of St. Stephen's Walbrook, London

Edited by Rev. Don Kistler

Soli Deo Gloria Publications
. . . for instruction in righteousness . . .

Soli Deo Gloria Publications
P.O. Box 451, Morgan, PA 15064
(412) 221–1901/FAX 221–1902

*

The Fight of Faith: The Remaining Sermons of Thomas Watson
is © 1996 by Don Kistler and Soli Deo Gloria.

*

ISBN 1–57358–047–3

Contents

Publisher's Note

Thomas Watson is one of the most beloved of the 17th century English Puritans. His writings and sermons are in constant demand. Nearly all of his sermons and treatises are in print at the present time. The Banner of Truth Trust began this important work by reprinting *The Beatitudes, The Lord's Prayer,* and *The Ten Commandments.* They have also published *Repentance* and *The Godly Man's Picture Drawn with a Scripture Pencil.*

Blue Banner Publications has published a rare Watson treatise on Malachi 3:16 entitled *Religion Our True Interest.*

Soli Deo Gloria has published many more of Watson's works, including *The Art of Divine Contentment, The Duty of Self-Denial, A Plea for the Godly, Heaven Taken by Storm, The Mischief of Sin,* and a collection first published in 1826 as *The Works of Thomas Watson,* which we have retitled *The Sermons of Thomas Watson.* There is also a collection of short sayings by Watson entitled *Gleanings from Thomas Watson.*

In compiling this collection, and by comparing the material now in print with the National Union Catalogue and the Short Title Catalogue, these sermons constitute the remaining sermons of Thomas Watson. There are two treatises yet to be published (*Jerusalem's Glory* and *The Two Witnesses Anatomized*), but, as far as we have been able to discern, these are the remaining "sermons" of Watson's that had yet to be reprinted. The last one, "The One Thing Necessary," was previously published in our compilation, *The Puritans on Conversion.*

The Crown of Righteousness

Set Forth in a Sermon Preached at St. Stephen's
Walbrook, May 1, 1656, at the Funeral
of Thomas Hodges, Esquire

"They that honor Me, I will honor."
1 Samuel 2:30

Dedication

To the virtuous, and my worthy friend,
Mrs. Mary Hodges

Honored Friend,

It was not my intention when I preached this sermon that it should go any further than the pulpit. But seeing you were pleased to request me to print it, that I might herein gratify your desire and exhibit testimonial of that respect which I bore to your deceased husband, I was willing to make it more public, and may the Lord make it profitable. You are sensible enough, I doubt not, of the late loss you have sustained. I therefore chose to treat this subject that I might revive you with the hope of future gain, not forgetting that saying in Proverbs 31:6, "Give wine to those that be of heavy heart."

The Jews have this form of speech at their funerals whereby they would cheer up the surviving party: "Let thy consolation be in heaven." So I say to you, look up to heaven. Let the crown laid up comfort you. The Lord help you to make a sanctified use of this sad stroke of providence.

Learn, dear friend, to make sure of Christ when you cannot make sure of other relations. Faith will contract you to Christ, and if your Maker is your Husband, death shall not dissolve but perfect the union. Labor still to anchor within the veil; 'tis no casting anchor downward. We break our earthly comforts while we lean too hard on them, but I must not expatiate.

I have here presented you with the sermon as I preached it, only I have cast in some few additional things which, through straits of time, I was then forced to omit. The blessing of the Almighty rest upon you, and let that golden oil be poured out upon your posterity. So prays,

Your faithful friend and servant in the Lord,

Thomas Watson

From my study at St. Stephen's, Walbrook
June 2, 1656

The Crown of Righteousness

"Henceforth there is laid up for me a crown of righteousness, which the Lord, the righteous Judge, shall give me at that day."
2 Timothy 4:8

The wise God, that He may invite and encourage the sons of men to holiness of life, is pleased to set before their eyes the recompense of reward, that if the equity of His precepts does not prevail, the excellency of His promise may. God will have His people to be volunteers in religion, not forced with fear but drawn with love. Therefore He works upon them in such a way as is most alluring and persuasive. He would catch men with a golden bait and tempt them to obedience by showing them what is laid up in heaven for them. So says the text, "Henceforth there is a crown of righteousness laid up. . . ." A crown? Oh, infinite! For a delinquent to have a pardon is well, but to have a crown set upon him is no less rare than stupendous.

A true saint has a double crown—one in this life, the other laid up. In this life he has a crown of acceptance. Ephesians 1:6: "He hath made us accepted in the Beloved." Some render it, "He hath made us favorites." Here is the crown of acceptance, and in

5

the life to come a crown of righteousness.

The glory of heaven is represented in Scripture under various similes and metaphors. Sometimes heaven is compared to a place of rest, as in Hebrews 4:9; it is the soul's center. Sometimes it is compared to a house not made with hands (2 Corinthians 5:1). Sometimes it is compared to an inheritance in light (Colossians 1:12), and in our text the glory of heaven is set forth by a crown.

The circle is the most perfect figure. This blessed crown encircles within it all perfection. I shall first break up the ground of the text by explication, and then come to sow the seed of doctrine.

"Henceforth." This word is a relative word. Either, first, it may bear date from the time of the Apostle's conversion—*henceforth* there is laid up a crown. As soon as a man is implanted into Christ, he stands entitled to a crown. Or, second, this word henceforth may relate to the end of his race and fight. Paul had run through all the several stages of Christianity. He had finished his course, and from henceforth, he said, there was laid up a crown. He knew his work was done, and there was nothing now remaining but to step out of the world and put on his crown.

"There is laid up for me a crown of righteousness."

QUESTION. Why a crown of righteousness? It is a crown of mercy, a crown that free grace bestows. Why, then, is it called a crown of righteousness?

ANSWER 1. Negatively, not that we can, by our righteousness, merit this crown. Bellarmine built his doctrine of merit on this text. Aquinas and

Bonaventure say that we merit this crown by way of condignity. But the whole current of our orthodox divines runs another way. And the Apostle makes a clear distinction between a reward bestowed by merit and by grace. Romans 6:23: "The wages of sin is death, but the gift of God is eternal life." Had the reward been by merit, the Apostle would have said, "The *wages* of God is eternal life." Alas! How can we merit a crown? Before we merit we must satisfy; but we have nothing to satisfy. How can finite obedience satisfy infinite justice? Besides, what equality is there between our service and the reward? What proportion is there between the shedding of a tear and the receiving of a crown? So we cannot, by our righteousness, merit this crown.

2. Affirmatively, it is called a crown of righteousness in a double sense. First, because it is a crown promised. Revelation 2:10: "I will give thee a crown." Since God made this promise, it is a righteous thing to bestow this crown on us. Second, it is a crown of righteousness because it is a crown purchased. It is a crown bought with the price of blood. It was so bought as it was given, else where was God's mercy? And it was so given as it was bought, else where was God's justice? This crown swims to us through the blood of a Savior. When Christ was hanging upon the cross, He was purchasing a crown for us. And in this sense it is a crown of righteousness. It is righteous with God to give us the crown which Jesus Christ has paid for so dearly.

3. This crown is said to be "laid up." The crown is kept in reversion. God does not presently broach the full vessels of glory. He does not presently install us

into our honor. It is a crown laid up. The saints are
heirs under age. God does not crown them until
they are of age. The sons of kings are often crowned
during their minority, some have been crowned in
the cradle, but the heirs of glory must be of perfect
stature before they are crowned. God will give His
children the ring and the bracelets here, some of
the comforts of His Spirit, but not the crown. We are
all for immediate pay. We are still putting off our repentance, yet would be putting on our crown. God
will have us stay awhile. The crown is "laid up."

QUESTION. But why is it laid up? Why is not the
crown presently put on?

ANSWER 1. It is not fit that we should yet wear it
for two reasons:

1. Our graces are imperfect in this life. They are
in their infancy and minority. Therefore we are said
to receive but "the first fruits of the Spirit" (Romans
8:23), not all of them, said Luther. We have only
some imperfect linaments of grace drawn in us. Our
graces are mingled with much corruption, as gold
in the ore is mingled with dross. The most refined
soul has some lees and dregs of sin left in it. The life
of grace is said to be hidden (Colossians 3:3). Our
faith is hidden under unbelief as the corn is hidden
under the chaff. Now if God should set this crown
upon us in this life, He would be crowning our sins
as well as our graces. Therefore, the crown is laid up.

2. It is not fit that we should yet wear the crown,
for then it would take us away from doing our work.
We would be idle in the vineyard. Who will take
pains for a reward when he has the reward already?
Therefore, the crown is laid up. We must run the

race before we wear the crown.

ANSWER 2. The crown is laid up to make heaven sweeter. The longer we wait for our crown, the sweeter it will be when it comes. The absence of that which we desire merely endears it more to us when we enjoy it. After all our sweating for heaven, all our praying, weeping, fasting, how welcome will a crown be? Therefore God, though He will not deny, will delay our reward. It is a crown laid up.

QUESTION. But if this crown is laid up, when shall we wear it?

ANSWER. This brings me to the fourth and last particular in the text.

"In that day." What day? In the day of my death, said Tertullian. Justinus and others are of the opinion that the saints shall not receive this crown until the resurrection. But Jerome confutes this opinion. The souls of the elect shall be immediately crowned with joy and felicity. The body, indeed, shall lie in the grave as in a bed of perfume until the resurrection. That this resurrection shall be is clear. Therefore it is that some of the ancients have called the grave a sleeping house because this body shall wake again. The Jews called their burying place the house of the living because they believed that life would come into them again at the resurrection. Till then, the bodies of the saints must wait for their preferment, but their souls shall be immediately crowned after death.

Why else would Paul desire to be dissolved if he were not immediately crowned with glory? It would be better for believers to stay here if they would not be immediately with Christ. Here they are daily im-

proving their stock of grace; they are increasing the
jewels of their crown. Though they sit in the valley
of tears, yet God often turns their water into wine.
They have many sweet tastes of God's love; they have
the bunches of grapes. If Paul's soul should sleep in
his body (a drowsy opinion), then when he desired
to be dissolved he wished that which was to be his
loss. But this crown shall be given "in that day," the
day of our death. It cannot be half a day's journey between the cross and paradise.

The words fall into these three parts:

1. Here is a glorious reward: a crown.

2. The adjourning of this reward: it is laid up.

3. The persons on whom it is bestowed: Paul and
the rest of the believers. "For me, and not for me
only, but for all them that love Christ's appearing."

**DOCTRINE. The righteous person shall wear the
crown of righteousness.**

For the illustration of this I shall do four things:

1. I shall inquire who this righteous person is.

2. I shall evidence by Scripture that the righteous
person shall wear this blessed crown.

3. I shall show you wherein this reward of glory is
compared to a crown.

4. I shall show you wherein the crown of righteousness excels and outshines all earthly crowns.

1. *Who this righteous person is.* A man may be said to
be righteous in two ways:

First, legally. Thus Adam, while he wore the robe
of innocence, was legally righteous. He had that law
of holiness written in his heart, and his life was a
living commentary on it. He went exactly, according

to every institute of God, like a well-made dial goes
with the sun; but this is lost and forfeited.

Second, evangelically. And this righteousness is
two-fold. There is a righteousness by imputation.
This is as truly ours to justify as it is Christ's to give.
Or there is a righteousness by implantation. The
one is by the merit of Christ, the other is by the
Spirit of Christ. Now this implanted righteousness is
in the soul as an intrinsic quality; and if it is of the
right kind it must be there in three ways.

(1) Righteousness must be in the soul exten-
sively, in every part. We do not call a black man
white because he has white teeth. Those are not said
to be righteous who only speak righteously. What
are these but white teeth? Righteousness, like a holy
leaven, must diffuse and swell itself into every part,
the understanding, will, and affections. "The very
God of peace sanctify you wholly" (1 Thessalonians
5:23). Therefore grace is called "the new man," not a
new eye or a new tongue, but a new man. Though a
saint is righteous but in part, yet he is righteous in
every part.

(2) Righteousness must be in the soul inten-
sively. We call water hot when it is hot in the third
or fourth degree. He is not said to be righteous who
is tepid and neutral in religion. This was Laodicea's
temper, lukewarm. Revelation 3:16: "I would thou
wert cold or hot." It is as if God said, "I wish you were
anything but lukewarm." Righteousness must rise
up to some degree. David boiled over in holy zeal.
Psalm 119:139: "My zeal hath consumed me."

(3) Righteousness must be in the soul perse-
veringly. It must abide and continue. He is not a

righteous person who is good only in a passion, either of fear or joy. Hypocrites may seem righteous for a time, as long as the wind sets that way, but it is quickly over. They change quickly, not unlike the herb whose leaves in the morning are white, at noon are purple, and at night are blue. Thus they change in their goodness and are of divers minds, like Joseph's coat of divers colors. Hypocrites, for the most part, live to confute themselves. They are like Cataline, of whom Sallust observes that he had a good and hopeful beginning, but a bad end. I have read of a certain people in India called Pandorae, who have white hoary hair in their youth and black hair in their old age. This is an emblem of hypocrites, who at first look white and fair like saints, but in their elder years blacken in wickedness. These men's religion was never ingrained. They are only to be judged righteous persons who, with Job, hold their integrity (Job 2:3).

There is a great deal of difference between the motion of a watch and the beating of a pulse. The one is quickly at an end, but the other, proceeding from a vital principle, is permanent and constant. As long as there is life the pulse beats. True righteousness is a spiritual pulse which will ever be beating. So much for the first point, who this righteous person is.

2. *The righteous person shall wear the crown of righteousness.* James 1:12: "He shall receive the crown of life." And Revelation 2:10: "I will give thee the crown of life." By both Scriptures you see that a true saint is an heir to the crown. The truth being so apparent, I

may say, as they did in another sense, "What need we any further witness?" (Luke 22:71). I proceed therefore to the next point.

3. *I will show you wherein the reward of glory is compared to a crown.* It is called here a crown of righteousness, and that in three respects:

A crown is resplendent. The royal crown, hung with jewels, is a splendid, magnificent thing. Thus the crown of righteousness is most radiant and illustrious. For the splendor of it, it is called a crown of glory (1 Peter 5:4). It must be glorious because it is a crown of God's own making. Sin has made us our crosses; God has made us our crown. What are all the beauties and glories of the world which have been esteemed most famous in comparison to this crown of righteousness? The Temple of Diana, Mausoleus' Tomb, the Egyptian Pyramids, the Pillar of the Sun, which the heathens offered to Jupiter, all fade by comparison. The glory of this crown is inexpressible. Were the angels themselves sent to heaven to give us a description of this crown of righteousness, they would sooner lack words than matter. But here I must draw a veil, as not being able to give you the dark shadow of it. Nor can it be set out by all the lights of heaven though every star were turned into a sun.

A crown is a weighty thing. So is the crown of righteousness. Therefore it is called a weight of glory by the Apostle. We think our sufferings are weighty; alas, they are light in comparison with our crown. This crown of righteousness is so weighty that it would soon overwhelm us if God did not make us able to bear it.

A crown is an honorable thing. "Thou crownest him with honor" (Psalm 8:5). Therefore, when King Ahasuerus asked Haman what should be done to the man whom the king would honor, Haman could think of nothing more honorable than the crown. "Let the crown royal which the king useth to wear be set upon his head" (Esther 6:8). A crown is not fit for everyone. It will not fit every head; it is for kings and persons of renown to wear. What a great honor it was to wear the Olympic crown, to which the Apostle here seems to allude. A crown is a badge and sign of imperial honor. So this crown of righteousness is the sign of royalty and excellence. Only those who are born of God and have the royal blood of heaven running in their souls wear this blessed crown. The men of the world may heap up silver like dust, but the crown God reserves only for those whom He has made kings (Revelation 1:6).

4. *The last thing is to show you wherein this crown of righteousness exceeds and outshines all earthly crowns.* This will appear in six particulars.

(1) This crown of righteousness is lawfully come by. It is a crown which God Himself will set upon our head. "The Lord, the righteous Judge will give it to me at that day," says the text. Therefore it is come by lawfully. Other crowns are often usurped, as history abundantly witnesses. They may be called crowns of unrighteousness because they are unrighteously gotten. Julius Caesar was wont to say that for a crown it was lawful to violate any oath. The saints do not have their crown by usurpation but by elec-

tion. They are chosen to a crown.

(2) This crown of righteousness exceeds in pureness. Other crowns are of a more foul, drossy metal; they have their troubles. A crown of gold cannot be made without thorns. Herein the crown of righteousness excels. It is made of a purer metal; there are no crosses or crowns woven into it. It fills the soul with melody; it banishes all sorrow from the heart; there can be no more sorrow in heaven than joy in hell.

(3) This crown of righteousness can never be lost or forfeited. Other crowns may be lost. "The crown is fallen from the head" (Lamentations 5:16). Henry VI was honored with the crowns of two kingdoms, France and England. The first was lost through the faction of his nobles; the other was twice plucked from his head before his death.

The crown has many heirs and successors. How many have been disposed either by fraud or force? But this crown of righteousness can never be lost. God will not say, "Remove the diadem, take off the crown" (Ezekiel 21:26). This crown is set upon the head of Christ's spouse, and Christ will never depose His spouse. There's nothing but sin that can forfeit the crown; but believers shall be so fixed in their orb of sanctity that they cannot have the least erring or retrograde motion.

(4) This crown of righteousness is a never-fading crown. Other crowns are like a garland of flowers that soon withers. "Doth the crown endure to all generations?" (Proverbs 27:24). All outward glory passes away as a swift stream or a ship in full sail. Crowns wear away and tumble into the dust, but the

crown of righteousness does not fade (1 Peter 5:4). Eternity is a jewel of the saint's crown. After millions of years, it will be as bright and resplendent as the first day's wearing.

(5) This crown of righteousness does not draw envy to it. David's own son envied him and sought to take his crown from off his head. A crown of gold is often the mark for envy and ambition to shoot at; but this crown of righteousness is free from envy. The white lily of peace is a flower that grows in this crown. One saint in glory shall not envy another because all are crowned. And though one crown may be larger than another, yet everyone shall have as big a crown as he is able to carry.

(6) This crown of righteousness makes a man blessed. Earthly crowns have no such virtue in them. They rather make men cursed. They are so heavy that they often sink men into hell. They make men's heads so giddy that they stumble and fall into hurtful lusts. But this crown of righteousness makes them blessed who wear it. The Hebrew word for "to crown" signifies "to compass round." Because the crown compasses those who wear it with terrestial felicity, the saints shall have a sight of God to eternity. This is the encompassing crown. The schoolmen place happiness in the vision of God. But besides, the saints shall have such communications of divine excellencies as they are capable of taking in. This is the quintessence of blessedness.

USE 1. OF INFORMATION. And there are four branches:

BRANCH 1. It shows us that religion is not im-

posed upon hard terms. God does not put us upon
unreasonable things. He does not give us work and
then give us no reward. Behold, there is a crown of
righteousness laid up. When we hear of the doctrine
of repentance, steeping our souls in briny tears for
sin, the doctrine of mortification, calling out the
right eye, we are ready to cry out as they did, "This is
a hard saying, who can hear it?" No, beloved, God's
terms are not unreasonable. He never sets us on
work but we are sure of double pay. He gives us many
sweet encouragements while we are doing the work.
He often strews our ways with roses, "shedding His
love abroad in our hearts" (Romans 5:5), filling us
with joy in believing (Romans 15:13).

He who has the least mercy from God in this way
will die in His debt. But when we look upon the recompense of reward, which as far exceeds our
thoughts as it surpasses our deserts, then surely we
cannot say to God (without wrong), as the man said
in Matthew 25:24, "I knew thee that thou art a hard
man." If a king should bid one take up his staff
when it is fallen, and for that should settle an annu-
ity upon him for life, would this not be unreasonable? When you have done all, as our Lord Christ
said, you are but unprofitable servants (Luke 17:10).
What advantage do you bring to God? Yet for this
poor, inconsiderable nothing there is a crown laid
up. Surely God does not invite you to your loss; nor
can you say He is a hard master. Will Satan, who
would discourage you from a strict, holy life, give
bond to assure you of something equivalent to this
crown? Saul said in another sense, "Will the son of
Jesse give you fields and vineyards, and make you

captains of thousands?" So, will Satan, who disparages the ways of God, give you crowns to possess?
Will he mend your wages? Alas! You know what
wages he pays. His wages are death, and truly, the
less of those wages the better.

BRANCH 2. See here that which may raise in our
hearts a holy indignation against sin, which makes
us forfeit our crown. Sin is not only hateful in its
own nature, but it is the most horrid, ugly, deformed
thing. This made holy Anselm say that if he should
behold the pains of hell on one side and the defor-
mity of sin on the other, and he must of necessity
choose one of these two, he said, "I would rather
throw myself into hell than voluntarily commit one
sin against God."

But besides the intrinsic filth that is in sin (it being the very spirit and quintessence of evil), this may
cause in us an abhorrence of it: Sin would degrade
us of our honor; it would pluck away our crown from
our head. Think what the end of sin will be. As
Abner said to Joab, "Will it not be bitterness in the
latter end?" (2 Samuel 2:26). If men, before they
committed sin, would but sit down and rationally
consider whether the present gain and sweetness in
sin would make amends for the future loss, I believe
it would put them into a cold sweat and give some
check to their unbridled affections. Jacob took Esau
by the heel. Oh, do not look upon the smiling face
of sin, but take it by the heel! Look at the end of it. It
will bereave us of our crown. And can anything
countervail this loss?

When a man is tempted to pride, let him remember that this will swell his head so big that the

crown will not go on. Woe to the crown of pride!
Isaiah 28 tells us that the crown of pride will hinder
him from the crown of righteousness. When he is
tempted to lust, let him remember that for enjoying
the pleasures of sin for a season he hazards a crown
for immorality. And is there as much sweetness in
sin as in a crown? When he is tempted to drunkenness (a sin that not only unChristians him but
unmans him), let him consider here that it would
uncrown him of his reason, and afterwards uncrown
him of his happiness. When he is tempted to swear-
ing, let him think with himself, "This is a sin which
has nothing to render it delightful." Other sins have
a show of pleasure and profit, which is the bait men
are drawn with, but the swearer is brought to the
devil's hook without any bait.

Oh! Is it not madness for these unfruitful works
of darkness to forfeit heaven? How will the devil reproach and laugh at men! That they should be so
stupid as to forego a crown for a rattle. They are like
those Indians who, for pictures and glass beads, will
part with their gold. Oh! How should we hate sin,
which will take away our crown from us.

BRANCH 3. See here the misery of a wicked man.
Though he may flourish in his bravery while he
lives, yet when he dies he shall not have a crown of
righteousness, but chains of darkness. Death carries
him prisoner to hell; it leads him away to be crucified. The Egyptians, as Plutarch reports, at their
feasts brought in a death's-head with this motto:
"Look upon this, and proceed with your banquet."
For the sinner who sports himself with sin and
crowns himself with rosebuds in the midst of all his

mirth and music, here's a death's-head for him to look on. The day of death to him will not be a day of inauguration, but a day of execution. How can the wicked rejoice? Theophylact used to say, "His estate is miserable who goes laughing to hell." We may say of this laughter, "It is mad" (Ecclessiastes 2:2).

Suppose you saw a man sitting in a rotten chair. Underneath him was a burning fire; over his head a sword was hanging by a twine thread; and before him was a table spread with a variety of delicacies. Surely he would have but little stomach to eat, sitting in that danger. So it is with a sinner. His soul sits in his body as in a chair. Diseases, like worms, breed there. Under him hellfire is burning. Over his head is not a crown, but a sword of justice hanging. When death breaks this chair of the body, he falls into the fire, and this fire is unquenchable. A multitude of tears cannot extinguish it; length of time cannot annihilate it. Nor let the sinner expect any Charon to ferry him over that Stygian lake (as some have vainly fancied).

God has the keys of hell, and, besides, the damned are bound hand and foot (Matthew 22:13), so that there can be no coming out. Oh, that this might frighten and stop men in their wicked courses! When they are dying, the wicked must say to their souls, as the Emperor Hadrian, "O my poor wandering soul, where are you going? What will become of you?" There remains nothing for sinners but a "certain fearful looking for of judgment and fiery indignation" (Hebrews 10:27). God will not say to them, "Come hither and be crowned," but rather, "Go ye cursed."

BRANCH 4. It shows us, as in a Scripture glass, the happiness and nobility of a righteous person. In this life he wears a robe of righteousness, and after death he wears a crown of righteousness.

1. In his lifetime he wears a robe of righteousness (Isaiah 61:10). This is the righteousness of Christ in which he is looked upon as righteous as Christ Himself (2 Corinthians 5:21). We are made the righteousness of God in Him. It is not said that we are made the righteousness of angels, but of God.

2. After death he wears a crown of righteousness. This crown encircles all blessedness within it. The saints are not perfectly happy till death; then comes the crown. Here we are but candidates and expectants of heaven. This is but seed time. We sow the seed of prayer and water it with our tears; the golden harvest is yet to be reaped. The crown is laid up. When Croesus asked Solon who he thought happy, he told him of Tellus, a man who was dead. So a Christian is not perfectly happy till death; then the crown shall be put on. The Thracians used music in their funerals, and Theocritus observes that the heathens had their funeral banquet because of the felicity which they supposed the deceased parties to participate in. When the mantle of a believer's flesh drops off, then shall his soul ascend in a triumphant chariot, and the garland of glory shall be set upon his head.

USE 2. OF TRIAL. Examine yourselves whether you are the heirs of this crown.

QUESTION. But how may that be known?

ANSWER. By this: if you set the crown on Christ's

head while you live, He will set the crown on your
head when you die. Have you wisdom to manage
business of concern, strength to do duties, resist
temptations and bear burdens? You will not assume
or arrogate anything to yourselves, but let Christ
wear the crown. Thus Paul said in 1 Corinthians
15:10, "I labored more than they all, and yet not I."
This is the inscription on Christ's vesture and on
His thigh, "King of kings" (Revelation 19:16). We do
what in us lies to make Him King when we set the
crown of all upon His head. King Canutus
(historians relate) took the crown off his own head
and set it upon a crucifix. So a good Christian takes
the crown of honor and applause from his own head
and sets it upon the head of Christ. This is hard for
flesh and blood to stoop to. A proud heart will not
easily part with the crown. He will command Christ
and bid others bow the knee. Only "in the throne he
would be greater," Genesis 41:40. But be assured,
there's no way for us to reign with Christ but to let
Christ reign here.

USE 3. OF EXHORTATION. This exhorts us to
four things.
1. If there is a crown laid up, it calls for our love
toward God. "Behold what manner of love the
Father hath bestowed upon us" to give us a crown.
This is the highest ennobling of a creature. If there
is love in a crumb, what is there in a crown? If there
is love in pardoning mercy, what is there in crowning mercy? It is a favor that we poor vermin, worms
and not men, should be allowed to live; but that
worms should be made kings, that Christ should be

arraigned and we adorned, that the curse should be laid on His head and the crown on ours— "Behold, what manner of love is this!" It is beyond all hyperbole. And should this not make our hearts reverberate and echo back love? Oh, Christians! Light your love at this fire; like burning glasses, they burn when the sun has shone on them. God having shone upon us in love, let our hearts burn, and our love to God must be divinely qualified.

First, it must be a genuine love. We must not love Him for something else, as a man loves a potion for health's sake, but as a man loves sweet wine for itself. We must love God for those intrinsic excellencies in Him which are so alluring and amiable.

Second, it must be a voluntary love, else it is not love but coercion. It must come freely, like water from a spring. It must be a free-will offering, not like the paying of a tax.

Third, it must be an exuberant love. It must not be stinted; not a few drops, but a stream. It must, like the Nile, overflow the banks.

Fourth, it must be a transcendent love. It must be of no ordinary extraction, but a choice, inure, superlative love. We must not only give God the milk of our love, but the cream; not only the truth of it, but the spirits and quintessence. "I would cause thee to drink of spiced wine, of the juice of my pomegranates" (Song of Solomon 8:2). If the spouse has a cup which is more juicy and spiced, Christ shall drink of that.

Fifth, it must be a most intense, ardent love. The sun shines as much as it can; such must our love to God be. It must boil over, but never give over. What

unparalleled love has God shown us! Oh, Christian!
Answer love with love. In love we may, as Bernard
said, reciprocate with God. If God is angry, we must
not be angry again; but if God loves us, we must love
Him again. Oh, love God the Father who has made
this crown for us. Love God the Son who has bought
this crown for us. Love God the Holy Spirit who has
made us fit to wear this crown.

2. Let us pant and breathe after this happy condition. Does not the heir desire to be crowned? Here
we have a weight of sin; in heaven we shall have a
weight of glory. How should our souls be big with
desire to be gone hence? What is the world we so
dote on? 'Tis but a spacious pardon, and should we
not be willing to go out of prison to be crowned?
The bird desires to go out of the cage, though it is
made of gold. The academics compare the soul of
man to a fowl, mounting with her wings aloft. Every
saint is a true bird of paradise; he is ever flying up
towards heaven in ardent and zealous affection; he
longs to be out of this earthen cage of the body,
when with the Phoenix he shall receive his golden
crowns on his head, and shine in glory as the angels
of God. Tertullian observes that Scipio, when his father had told him of that glory the soul should be
invested with in a state of immortality, said Scipio,
"Why do I tarry thus long upon the earth? Why do I
not hasten to die?"

I think that, when we hear of this crown of righteousness which will so infinitely enrich and adorn
the soul, it should make us be weary of this world
and long for the time of our solemn inauguration.
How did Paul desire to be dissolved? Would not man

be willing to hoist up sails and cross the waters, though troublesome, if he were sure to be crowned as soon as he came ashore? Why are our souls so earthly? We love to be grazing in the world's full pastures, and are afraid to die. Most men look so ghastly at the thoughts of death, as if they were rather going to the cross than the crown. Oh, long for death! The Apostle calls death a putting off of our earthly clothes (2 Corinthians 5:4). This is all death does to us, if we are in Christ—it puts off our clothes and puts on a crown. This should make us say, as did Hilarion, "Go out, my soul, go out. Why do you tremble? You are going to receive a crown." A believer, at death, will be the happiest loser and the happiest gainer. He will lose his sins; he will gain glory. The day of death is the saint's coronation day.

3. Learn to deport and demean yourselves so that this crown of righteousness may be set upon your heads when you die.

QUESTION. How do we do that?

ANSWER. Do three things:

1. *If you would wear the crown of righteousness, find in your hearts the work of righteousness, Isaiah 32:17.* That is the work of grace wrought in you; and this work must be evidenced by a mighty change, which is sometimes called an engrafting, sometimes a transforming. Grace makes a metamorphosis; it produces in the soul a configuration and likeness to Christ. First there must be a consecrating work before a crowning work. We read in Scripture of the solemn inauguartion of their king. First they anointed them and then they crowned them. "Zadok the priest took a horn of oil out of the tabernacle, and anointed

Solomon" (1 Kings 1:39), and after that he was crowned. So there must be the unction of the Spirit: first God pours on us the anointing oil of grace, and after the horn of oil comes the crown.

2. *If you would wear the crown of righteousness, then walk in the way of righteousness (Proverbs 12:28).* This is called in Scripture a walking after the Spirit (Romans 8:1). The people of Israel walked after the pillar of fire and the wise men walked after the star; which way the star went, they went. And sometimes it is called a walking by rule (Galatians 6:16). Those who expect a golden crown must walk by a golden rule. Be sure you walk with David's candle and lantern in your hand (Psalm 119:105). He who walks in the dark may soon be out of the way. Walk soberly in acts of temperance, righteously in acts of justice, and godly in acts of piety. Walk as Christ did upon earth. His life was purer than the sunbeams, as one said. Copy His life in yours. Be assured you shall never partake of the privilege of Christ's death unless you imitate the pattern of Christ's life. Would you wear the crown of righteousness? Walk in the way of righteousness. But alas, this is a very untrodden way:

(1) Some know the way of righteousness but do not walk in it, like the Grecians of whom Plutarch speaks; they knew what was honest but did it not.

(2) Others commend the way of righteousness but do not walk in it, like those who taste and commend the wine but do not buy.

(3) Others walk like Antipodes instead of walking in the way. They are good only at crossing

the way; they oppose the way of righteousness. Such are persecutors (2 Timothy 3:8).

(4) Others walk a few steps in the way and then go back again. These are apostates (2 Timothy 4:10), as if there were any going to heaven backwards.

(5) Others walk half in the way and half out. These are loose professors who, though in some dogmatic things they differ from us, yet, under a notion of Christian liberty, walk carelessly and presumptuously, crying up justification so that they may weaken the power of sanctification. They can take that liberty which others tremble to think of. Surely, were there no other Bible read but the lives of some professors, we should read but little Scripture there.

(6) Others walk soberly awhile in the way, but all of a sudden, drinking in the poison of error, begin to be intoxicated with novel and dangerous opinions, who, as the Apostle said, "are turned aside after Satan" (1 Timothy 5:15). Ignatius calls error the invention of the devil. Basil calls it a spiritual drunkenness, and when the head is giddy the feet must reel. Loose principles breed loose practices.

(7) Others, instead of walking in the way, traduce and slander the way of righteousness. "The way of truth shall be evil spoken of" (2 Peter 2:2); or, as it is in the Greek, it shall be blasphemed. The men of the world give out that the way of righteousness is a solitary way and makes them melancholy who walk in it, and that they must expect to lose their joy by the way. These forget that golden saying of Augustine that when a man is converted and turned to God, his joy is not taken away but changed. 'Tis

more sublime and pure. And does not Solomon's oracle tells us that "all the ways of God are pleasantness" (Proverbs 3:17)? Take the most rugged part of the way of religion, and it is pleasant walking. Holy weeping seems at first very uncouth and disconsolate, but how often, while the saints weep for sin, does the Lord make them weep for joy? While the water of repentance, like rose-water, drops from the eye, it sends forth a sweet smell which refreshes the soul with inward consolation. Oh, what green branches! What full clusters of grapes hang all along as we are walking in the way of righteousness! How, then, dare men calumniate?

(8) Others creep in the way; they do not walk. They go on but very slowly, like the motion of the eighth sphere. Those who look on can hardly tell whether they make any progress or not. They are dull in their heavenly motion and need often to pray with David for God's free Spirit (Psalm 51:12).

(9) Others walk quite beside the way. These are profane persons who dedicate their lives to Bacchus, who border every step they take upon the devil's confines. They are like Asa, diseased in their feet. They walk, as the Apostle said, disorderly, like soldiers who march out of rank and file. Jesus Christ not only sends forth blood out of His sides to redeem us, but also water to cleanse us (1 John 5:6). They who do not have the power of the one to sanctify question the benefit of the other to save. Oh! All you who would wear the crown of righteousness, walk in the way of righteousness. Labor to keep up the credit of religion in the world. Walk exactly. Walk so that if we could suppose the Bible to be lost,

it might be found again in your lives.

3. *If you would wear the crown of righteousness, put on the armor of righteousness (2 Corinthians 6:7).* The meaning is this: if you will have this crown you must fight for it. Paul said, "I have fought the good fight," a metaphor, as Chrysostom and Ambrose observe, taken from wrestlers who, when they had gotten the victory, were crowned. 'Tis the crown of victory; therefore the saints in glory are set forth with palms in their hands in token of victory. Christians must strive like Olympian combatants. They must not only be adorned with the jewel of knowledge, but armed with the breastplate of faith. Satan is a lion in the way; there must be a pitched battle.

This crown is worth contending for. A Christian most shines in his spiritual armor. This is his sacred gallantry, when he is like those soldiers Curtius speaks of who did not look gay in gold and glittering apparel, but shone in their martial habit. The crown is set upon the head of the conqueror. Those dainty, silken Christians who live at ease, and will not make the least sally out against the enemy, shall have no crown, but will be discarded as cowards. Lycurgus would have no man's name written upon his sepulchre but he who died manfully in war. God will write no man's name in the book of life but he who dies fighting. When the saints, after all their spiritual battles, shall come to heaven as conquerors, then (as was said of Caesar) shall their ensigns of honor be hung up; then shall the crown of righteousness be set upon their head.

Let this put spurs to our sluggish hearts and make us act with all our might for God. What, wrestling? What, sweating? How should we provoke ourselves to holiness! How should we spend and be spent for Christ! How should we strive to bring in some crown revenues to our Lord and Master when we consider how infinitely it shall be rewarded! While we are laying out for God, He is laying up for us; henceforth there is a crown laid up. How should this crown add wings to prayer and oil to the flame of our zeal! O Christian, let your head study for Christ; let your tongue plead for Him; let your hands work for Him! "What honor and dignity hath been done to Mordecai?" said King Ahasuerus (Esther 6:3). Inquire what has been done for God. I think we should sometimes go aside into our closets and weep to consider how little work we have done for God. Beloved, what a vast disproportion there is between our work and our reward, between our sweat and our crown. And 'tis but awhile, a very little while, before the crown shall be put on. The time is short, said the Apostle. We are ready to strike sail; we are almost at shore; and then we shall be crowned. Oh! Improve the present season for the glory of God. The crown is hard by; you sail apace and work apace.

And that I may put spirits into Christians and quicken their obedience, consider this: the more work you do for God, the bigger crown you shall wear. There are degrees of glory. He who with his pound gained five more was made ruler over five cities. But he who with his pound gained ten was made ruler over ten cities. As one star differs from another in glory, so one crown differs from another in glory. If there are degrees of torment in hell, thereby, for the same reason, there are degrees of glory in heaven. That there are degrees of torments is evident from Luke 20:47: "Who for pretense make long prayers, the same shall receive greater damnation." They who wrap sin in a religious mantle, who entitle God to their wickedness, shall have a hotter place in hell. Even so there are gradations in happiness. How, then, should we abound in work, seeing we shall exceed in reward!

USE 4. OF CONSOLATION. Here is a gospel honeycomb, dropping comfort into the hearts of the godly. How may this alleviate all the afflictions of this life, and make these waters of Marah sweet and pleasant to drink of. There is a crown laid up. A Christian in this life has something to grieve him and yet something to comfort him. A true saint is an heir of the cross. If he wears any robes, they are bloody; if he wears any crown, 'tis one of thorns. But here is that which may sweeten his sufferings; here is wine mingled with his myrrh—he shall be crowned in paradise. This, my brethren, may change our mourning into melody and our tears into triumph. Though we bear the cross, we shall wear the crown; and these sufferings cannot continue long. If our life is short, our sufferings cannot be long. Oh, how may this sweeten all the bitter cups we drink of! Cleopatra put a jewel in her cup which contained the price of a kingdom. When we are drinking in our wormwood cup, let this jewel be put into our cup to make it go down more pleasantly. There's a reward of glory. Though death is in the cup, sugar lies at the bottom. Henceforth there is a

crown of righteousness laid up. So much for the
text; now to the occasion.

Sorry I am to be an actor in this mournful scene.
It might better have become some other (grief often
causing brokenness of expression), but I forbear to
apologize. We are here met to solemnize the funeral
of Thomas Hodge, Esquire, who, I believe, was not
more generally known than loved. I shall not be
such a Praeco as Homer of Achilles. What I shall
speak of him now interred shall be only some of my
own observations. I hate to give flattering titles;
only, seeing it is the last office of love I can do, suffer me to strew a few flowers upon his hearse. The
Jews embalmed the bodies of their dead, and why
may not names be embalmed?

1. He was not only a frequenter, but a very rever-
ent hearer of the Word. To my best observation, he
seemed to receive the truth not only in the *light* of it
but in the *love* of it.

2. He was a great zealot and opposed error. He
liked not to hear heterodox preachers, knowing that
smooth tongues could easily give out bad wares. He
was a friend to truth.

3. He was a great honorer and encourager of the
lawfully-ordained ministers. I seldom heard him
speak of such as were conscientious without some
testimony of respect. I observed that he ever prized
those ministers most (not who smoothed their
tongues, as in Jeremiah 23:31, or who used to jingle
out their words in the pulpit, whose preaching was
rather musical than medicinal, but) who spoke most
to the conscience. It was a good sign of a spiritual
appetite that he rather liked the savoriness of the

meat than the garnishing of the dish.

4. He was a most true-hearted man to his friends. He did not know that art which some have at the same time to flatter and hate. The Romans painted friendship with her hand upon her heart, a hieroglyphic emblem of a faithful friend who fetches all words from the bottom of his heart. Our deceased friend would speak plainly what was in his mind, not like those who have the honey of fair words in their mouth and the sting of malice in their heart.

5. He was one who did not sinfully comply with the humors of men. There are too many who, Proteus-like, can change into any shape, who can sail with any wind, especially if it blows preferment. This I may say of him: though death broke him, the times could never bend him. He often, in my hearing, blessed God for that liberal allowance which providence had carved out to him; nor did he desire to increase his estate by increasing his guilt.

6. He was very charitable to the poor. The age we live in, though it has the lamp of profession, yet it has little of the oil of charity. 'Tis the sin of many rich men that, though they have a flourishing estate, they have a withered hand and cannot stretch it out to good uses. It was a serious and weighty speech of Chrysostom, "Feed the hungry with your charity while you live that you feed not the fire of hell when you die."

There was a temple erected at Athens which they called the Temple of Mercy. It was dedicated to charitable uses. And there could not be a greater reproach laid upon any man than to upbraid him that he had not been in the Temple of Mercy. This may be the reproach of many rich men in this city: though they may sometimes visit God's temple in frequenting public ordinances, yet they are seldom or never seen in the temple of mercy. They can drink in a full cup themselves, but will not let one drop fall beside to refresh the bowels of the poor. Their arguments conclude still in Celarent. As for our deceased friend, let it be his garland now that he is gone. He had not only an estate but a heart. Though I often went to him for works of charity, he did not make any excuses (which are only handsome denials), but his fingers dropped with the myrrh of liberality, which is a sacrifice of a sweet-smelling savor to God.

He had, indeed, a free and noble spirit. He sailed equally between two rocks. He avoided vain profuseness; he hated a sordid penuriousness. When I came to him on his deathbed, he told me that sin was the burden of his life, and that he cast himself only on the merits of Christ. But, he said, "How hard I find it to believe," which words were dropped out with many tears. 'Tis better to complain than presume. I might expatiate, but I shall here contract my sails.

These things were commendable in him and may be imitated by us. Here was good fruit which adorned the tree. It will be our wisdom to copy out what we see good in others, and to walk so unblamably in holiness that while we live we may have good hope through grace of a part and interest in Christ, and when we die we may receive that crown of righteousness, "which the Lord the righteous judge shall give at that day to all them who love His appearing."

The Righteous Man's Weal and the Wicked Man's Woe

(Being the last sermon Watson preached at Clements-Danes, London, August 19, 1662, the Tuesday after his Farewell Sermon to his people at St. Stephen's, Walbrook)

The Righteous Man's Weal and the Wicked Man's Woe

"Say ye, surely it shall be well with the just
for they shall eat the fruit of their works.
Woe be to the wicked, it shall be ill with
him: for the reward of his hands shall
be given him." Isaiah 3:10–11

This text is like Israel's pillar or cloud—it has a light side and a dark side. It has a light side unto the godly ("Say unto the righteous it shall be well with him"), and it has a dark side unto the wicked ("Woe unto the wicked, it shall be ill with him"). Both, you see, are rewarded, righteous and wicked, but here is a vast difference: one has a reward of mercy and the other a reward of justice.

I begin with the first of these, "Say unto the righteous it shall be well with him." This Scripture was written in a very sad and calamitous time, as you may read in the beginning of the chapter: "The mighty man and the man of war shall cease, the prudent and the ancient, both judge and prophet shall be taken away." This was a very sad time with the church of God in Jerusalem.

If the judge is taken away, where will there be any

equity? If the prophet is removed, where will there
be any priests? The whole body politic was running
to ruin and almost in the rubbish. Now in this sad
juncture of time, God would have this text to be written; and it is like a rainbow in the clouds. God
would have His people comforted in the midst of all
afflictions. "Say unto the righteous it shall be well
with him."

The great proposition that lies in the words is
this: however things go in the world, it shall be well
with the righteous man. This is an oracle from
God's own mouth; therefore, we are not to dispute it.
It is God's own oracle, "Say unto the righteous it
shall be well with him."

I might multiply Scriptures, but I will give you
one instance in Ecclesiastes 8:12: "Surely I know that
it shall be well with them that fear God." I know it. It
is as a golden maxim not to be disputed. "It shall be
well with them that fear God."

For the illustration of this, consider two ques-
tions: Who is meant by "the righteous man"? And
what does it mean that, however things go, it shall
be well with the righteous?

QUESTION 1. Who is meant here by the righteous man?

ANSWER. There is a threefold righteousness:

1. There is a legal righteousness, and so Adam,
in this sense, was said to be righteous when he wore
the robe of innocence. Adam's heart agreed with
the law of God exactly as a well-made dial goes with
the sun; but this righteousness is forfeited and lost.

2. There is a moral righteousness, and thus he is
said to be righteous who is adorned with the moral

virtues, who is prudent and just and temperate, who is decked with the jewel of morality.

3. There is an evangelical righteousness and this is meant here. This evangelical righteousness is two-fold.

There is a righteousness of imputation, and that is when Christ's righteousness is made over to us. Beloved, this righteousness is as truly ours to justify us as it is Christ's to bestow upon us.

There is a righteousness of implantation, which is nothing else but the infusing of the seed and habit of grace into the heart, a planting of holiness in a man and making him partaker of the divine nature. This is to be righteous in the sight of God, a righteousness of imputation and a righteousness of implantation.

QUESTION 2. How is it that however things go in the world, yet it shall be well with this righteous man?

ANSWER. It must be thus for two reasons:

1. Because he who is righteous has his greatest evils removed, his sin pardoned, and then it must be well with him. Sin is the thorn in a man's conscience. When the thorn is plucked out by forgiveness and remission, then it is well with that man.

Forgiveness in Scripture is called a lifting off of sin. Job 7:21: "Lord, why dost not Thou lift off my sin?" So the Hebrew word carries it; it is a metaphor taken from a weary man who goes under a burden and is ready to sink under it, and then another man comes and lifts off this burden. Even so does the great God. When the burden of sin is ready to sink

the confidence, God lifts off this burden from the
conscience and lays it on Christ's shoulder and He
carries it now. He who has this burden thus carried,
it is well with him however things go.

Forgiveness of sin and pardon is a crowning
blessing. It is the jewel of a believer's crown. Pardon
of sin is a multiplying mercy and it brings a great
many mercies along with it. Whom God pardons, He
adopts; whom God pardons, He invests with grace
and glory.

This is a multiplying mercy and it is enough to
make a sick man well. Isaiah 33:24: "The inhabitants
shall not say, 'I am sick'; the people shall be for-
given their iniquity." The sense of pardon takes away
the sense of pain, and then it must be well with the
righteous for his greatest evil is removed.

2. However things go, it is well with the righteous
because God is his portion. Psalm 16:5–6: "The Lord
is the portion of my inheritance. The lines are
fallen unto me in pleasant places." In God, there are
all good things to be found; and all that is in God is
engaged for the good of the righteous. His power is
to help and His wisdom is to teach and His spirit is
to sacrifice and His mercy is to save.

God is the righteous man's portion, and can God
give a greater gift unto us than Himself? God is a
rich portion, for He is the angel's riches. God is a
safe and sure portion, for His name is a strong
tower. He is a portion that can never be spent for He
is infiniteness. He is a portion that can never be lost
for He is eternity. "Thou art my portion forever"
(Psalm 73:26), and surely it is well with the righteous
who has God for his portion. Is it not well with that

man who is happy? Why, if God is our portion, we are happy. Psalm 144:15: "Happy is the people whose God is the Lord."

Thus I have cleared up the doctrinal part for the use of this. Here is abundance of comfort for every godly man, for every person serving God in this congregation. God has sent me this day with a commission to comfort you.

Oh, that I might drop the oil of gladness into every broken heart and rejoice every troubled spirit. Here is good news from heaven: "Say unto the righteous it shall be well with him."

QUESTION 3. But here is a question that must be answered. You will say to me, "But how does it appear that it shall be well with the righteous, for we often see it is worse with them in this world? He is deprived of his comfort many times; he loses his very life in that quarrel and he is made the very reproach of the world oftentimes. How then is it well with the righteous?"

ANSWER. To this I answer, still it is well with the righteous. Though he meets with trouble in the world and one follows on the neck of another, yet it is well with the righteous as will appear in these four particulars:

1. The troubles the righteous man meets with turn to his good, and so it is well with him. That is a most famous Scripture in Jeremiah 24:5: "Whom I have sent out of this place unto the land of the Chaldeans for their good." God's own Israel was transported into Babylon among their enemies, but it is for their good, said the Lord; the troubles of the

righteous are a means to purge out their sin. I have
read a story of one who was running at another with
a sword to kill him, and by accident his sword ran
into an imposter and broke the imposter. Thus all
the evils and troubles of the righteous serve but to
cure them of the imposture of pride and to make
them more humble. When that body of a saint is afflicted, his soul revives and flourishes in grace.

At Rome, there were two laurel trees and when
one withered the other flourished. So when the body
is afflicted, the soul revives and flourishes.

God distills out of the bitterest drink His glory
for our salvation. Jerome said that the world looks
on it as a punishment, but God makes a medicine to
heal the sore. Then it is well with the righteous. The
rod of God upon a saint is but only God's pencil
whereby He draws His image more lively on the soul.
God never strikes the strings of His violin but to
make the music the sweeter. Then it is well with the
righteous.

2. In the midst of all the trouble that befalls the
righteous, still it is well with them in regard to those
inward heart revivings that God gives them. We see a
godly man's misery, but we do not see his comfort.
We see his prison gates, but we do not hear the music that is within his conscience. God sweetens His
people in outward trouble with inward peace. It is
what God is said to do in 2 Corinthians 7:6, comfort
those who are cast down. The bee can gather honey
as well from the thistle and bitter herb as from the
sweet flower. A child of God can gather joy out of his
sorrow. Out of the very carcass, sometimes, the Lord
gives honey. When the body is in pain, the soul may

be at ease. Just as when a man's head aches yet his heart may be well, thus it is well with the righteous. God gives him that inward comfort that revives and sweetens his outward pain.

3. In the time of trouble and calamity, yet still it is well with the righteous because God covers His people in time of trouble. He hides them in the storms. God cares to hide His jewels and will not let them be carried away; thus He makes good the Scripture, Psalm 91:4, 10: "He shall cover them with His feathers and under His wings shalt thou trust; no evil shall touch thee."

God oftentimes verifies this Scripture literally. He makes His angels to be His people's lifeguard to hide and defend them. When a flood was coming upon the world, God provided an ark to hide Noah. When Israel was carried and transported into Babylon, God hid Jeremiah and gave him his life for a prey, Jeremiah 39:11. In this sense, the saints of God are called hidden ones in Psalm 83:3. Why so? Not only because they are hidden in God's decree and Christ's wounds, but, oftentimes, God hides them in a time of common danger and calamity. They are hidden ones. He reserved to Himself 7,000 who had not bowed the knee to Baal. The prophet knew not where there was one, but God knew where there were 7,000. In this sense it is well with the righteous in time of public misery.

But you'll say, "Sometimes it fares worse than all this. Sometimes the righteous die and perish. They are carried away with a tempest. Why?"

Yet still it is well with the righteous, and that in a twofold sense:

(1) Many times God does take away the righteous by death and in great mercy, he takes them away that they shall not see the misery that comes upon a nation. Virgil, the heathen poet, said, "They are happy that die for their country." His meaning was they die before they see the ruin of their country. Truly God many times takes away His people in mercy that they may not see the ruin that is coming on a land. You have a Scripture for this in 1 Kings 14:13: "He only of Jeroboam shall come to the grave in peace because in him there is found some good things towards the Lord God of Israel." God puts him in this grave betimes in mercy because he should not see the evil coming on the land. There's a parallel to this in 2 Kings 12:21. It is spoken in Joshua, "I will gather thee unto thy Fathers, thou shalt be gathered unto thy grave in peace and thine eyes shall not see the evil I will bring upon this place." Joshua died in battle; how then was it said he went to the grave in peace? We must understand the meaning of it; Joshua went to his grave in peace because he was a holy man and he made his peace with God. Because he should not see the evil approaching, God gathered him to his grave in peace.

Jerome, speaking of his friend Nepotian (you must observe Jerome lived to see some troubles before he died), said, "Oh, how happy is my friend Nepotian, that sees not these troubles but is got out of the storm and is arrived safe in the haven."

Luther died in mercy before the troubles in Germany broke forth. Thus you see that it is well with the righteous, though they die. God takes them away in mercy that they may not see approaching evils.

(2) Though the righteous die and are taken away, it is well with them because death cannot hurt them. Death can neither hurt their bodies nor their souls, and it is well with them.

Death cannot hurt their bodies. The body of a saint does not perish though it die. The bodies of the saints are very precious dust in God's account. The Lord locks up these jewels in the grave as in a cabinet. The bodies of the saints lay mellowing and ripening in the grave until the blessed time of the resurrection. Oh, how precious is the dust of a believer! Though the world minds it not, yet it is precious to God.

The husbandman has some corn in his barn and other corn in the ground. Why? The corn that is in the ground is as precious to him as that in the barn. The bodies of the saints in the grave are God's corn in the ground, but the Lord makes very precious account of this corn. The bodies of the saints shall be more glorious and blessed at the resurrection than ever they were before. Tertullian calls them angelic bodies with regard to the beauty and luster that shall be upon them. This is as it is with your silks—when they are dyed a purple or scarlet color, they are made more bright and illustrious than they were before. Thus it is with the bodies of the saints—they shall be dyed a better color at the resurrection and shall be made like a glorious body (Philippians 3:20). Thus it shall be well with the righteous; their bodies shall not perish.

4. It will be well with the righteous at death as to

their souls, too. Oh, it will be a blessed time! I think
it is with a saint at the time of death just as it was
with St. Paul in his voyage to Rome, where we read
that the ship broke, but though there were so many
broken pieces, he got safely to shore. Though the
ship of the believer's body breaks by death, it is safe
with the passenger; his soul gets safely to the heavenly harbor. Let me tell you, the day of a believer's
death is the birthday of his blessedness. It is his ascension day to heaven. It is his marriage day with
Jesus Christ. Faith contracts us here in this life, but
at death the nuptials shall be solemnized in glory.
They shall see God face to face. It will be heaven
enough to have a sight of God, said Augustine.
When the saints enter into joy here, joy enters into
them; but then they shall enter into it. They shall
drink of those pure rivers that run from the everlasting fountain.

Thus, you see it will be well with the righteous.
However things go, though trouble comes, though
death comes, it will go well with the righteous. Oh,
let those who are the people of God comfort themselves with these words! What an encouragement
this is to all you who hear me to begin to be righteous. This text may tempt us all to be godly. "Say
unto the righteous it shall be well with him." When
things are never so ill with him, yet it is well with
him.

We would be glad to have things go well within
our relations and in our estates. Why? When these
righteous things go well with us, your person is
sealed. You are heir of all God's promises; you are
Christ's favorite; you have heaven in reversion; and

is it not now well with you? If you would have happiness, you must espouse holiness. Say unto the righteous it shall be well with them, and this much of the first proposition, of the godly man's comfort in life and death: it is well with him.

But now, if all this will not prevail with you to make you leave your sins and become righteous, I must pass on a few words to the next branch of the text to scare men out of their sins, to frighten men out of their wickedness: "Woe unto the wicked, it shall be ill with him."

This, my beloved, is the dark side of the cloud. It may cause in every wicked man who hears me a trembling at the heart. "Woe unto the wicked, it shall be ill with him." The proposition resulting out of the words is this: When things seem to be well with the wicked, it shall be ill with them at last. Though they have more than their heart can wish, yet it shall be ill with them at last. Ecclesiastes 8:13: "It shall not be well with the wicked, nor shall he prolong his days which are as a shadow because he fears not God." It shall not be well with the wicked; the God of truth has pronounced this.

It is as true as God is true, it shall not be well with the wicked. Now that I may make this a little clearer to you, I shall demonstrate this to you in these four particulars:

1. It is ill with the wicked in this life.
2. It is ill with them at death.
3. It is ill with them at the day of judgment.
4. It is ill with them after judgment; it shall be ill with the wicked.

1. *It is ill with the wicked in this life.* A wicked man
who hears me will hardly think so when he has the
affluence and confluence of outward comforts,
when he eats the fat and drinks the sweet. He will
hardly believe the minister who tells him it shall be
ill with him; but it is so. For is it not ill with that
man who has a curse? Yea, the curse of God is entailed upon him, and can that man ever thrive who
lives under the curse of God?

Floods of blood and wrath hang over the head of
a wicked man. He is heir to all the plagues written
in the Book of God. All God's curses are the sinner's
portion, and, if he dies in his sin, he is sure to have
his portion paid him.

Woe unto the wicked! Every bit of bread he has,
he has it with a curse. It is like poisoned bread given
to a dog. Every drop of wine he drinks, he swallows a
curse with it. Woe unto the wicked! There is a curse
in his cup and upon his table. God said, "Woe unto
him." We read of Belshazzar, in Daniel 5:2-4, that he
took the wine and commanded to bring the gold
and silver vessels out of the temple. Then they
brought the golden vessels that were taken out of
the temple, out of the house of God that was in
Jerusalem, and the king, his princes, his wives, and
his concubines drank from them.

Belshazzar was jovial in the midst of his cups. He
was merry. But woe unto the wicked, for in the same
hour came forth the finger of a man's hand and
reached over the candlestick upon the plaster of the
wall of the king's palace; and the king's countenance changed and he was troubled. There was a
hand and a woe written on the wall. Let a sinner live

till he comes to a hundred years of age, yet he is cursed (Isaiah 65:20). His gray hairs have a curse upon them.

2. *It is ill with the wicked not only in this life, but at the hour of death in these two respects:* (1) Death puts an end to all his comforts and (2) death is the beginning of all his miseries.

1. Death puts an end to all his comforts—no more indulging and pampering the flesh, no more cups of wine, no more music. Revelation 18:14, 22: "The fruits thy soul lusted after are departed from thee. All things that are dainty and good are departed from thee; the voice of the harpist, musician, and trumpeter shall be heard no more in thee."

It is spoken of the destruction of Rome. And so you may say of the wicked man, no more joy and gladness, no more mirth and music. All a sinner's sweet spices, his scarlet robes, his sparkling diamonds, all depart from him at death.

2. As death puts an end to a sinner's mirth, so it lays a foundation for all his sorrow. Alas, before death begins to close a sinner's eyes, the eye of his conscience is first opened. Every sin at the hour of death stands with its drawn sword in its hand. Those sins that delighted him in life now frighten and terrify him. All his joy and mirth turn into sadness as sometimes you have seen sugar lying in a damp place, dissolving and running to water. Thus all the sugared joys of a wicked man at the hour of death turn into the water of tears and into the water of sorrow.

3. *It shall be ill with the wicked man at the day of judgment when he is seated before God's tribunal.* He shall leave

judging others and shall stand at God's bar and be
tried for his life.

I read that when Felix heard Paul speak of judgment he trembled. Josephus observed that Felix was
a wicked man, and the woman who lived with him,
Drusilla, he enticed from her husband and lived in
uncleanness with her. Now when Felix heard Paul
preaching of judgment he trembled. Now if he
trembled to hear of judgment, what will he do when
judgment comes, when all his secret sins shall be
made manifest, and all his midnight wickedness
shall be written on his forehead as with the point of
a diamond? At the day of judgment shall be two
things: first, there shall be a legal trial; second, the
sentence.

First, a legal trial. God will call forth the sinner
by name and say, "Stand forth, hear your charge, see
what you can answer to this charge! What can you
say for your Sabbath-breaking, your murders, your
drunkenness and perjury? For all your revenge and
malice? For all the persecuting of My members?
What do you say, guilty or not guilty? You wretch,
you dare not say you are not guilty, for have I not
been an eyewitness to all your wickedness? Do not
the books agree, the book of your conscience and
the book of My omniscience, and dare you offer to
plead not guilty?" How will the sinner be amazed
with horror and run in desperation!

Second, after this legal process or trial follows
the sentence: "Go ye cursed into everlasting fire." Go
from the presence of Christ, in whose presence is
fullness of joy; go from Christ with a curse. Why, said
Chrysostom, that very word "depart" is worse than

the torment itself. Remember this, you who go on in your sins, once this sentence is passed it can never be reversed. This is the most supreme court of judicature, from which there is no appeal. Here on earth men remove their causes from one court to another, from the common-law court into the chancery. But, at the last day of judgment, there will be no appeals and no removing the sentence, for this is the highest court.

4. *It will be ill with the wicked who die in their sins after the day of judgment.* Then there is but one way, and they would be glad if they might not go that way, any way but to prison. Oh, but there is no way but to hell. Luke 16:23: "In hell he lifted up his eyes." Hell is the very center of misery; it is the very spirit of torments distilled out. The Scripture tells us that in hell there are these three things: fire, darkness, and chains.

(1) Hell is called a place of darkness. Jude 13: "To whom is reserved blackness of darkness." Darkness, you know, is the most uncomfortable thing in the world. A man who goes in the dark trembles every step. Hell is a black region, nothing but blackness of darkness. It must be a dark place where they shall be separated from the light of God's presence. Indeed, Augustine thinks there shall be some little sulphurous light there; but even if it is so, that light will serve only that the damned may see the tragedy of their own misery and see themselves tormented.

(2) In hell, as there is darkness so there is fire. It is called a burning lake in Revelation 20:15: "Who was not found written in the Book of Life was thrown into the lake of fire." You know that fire is

the most torturing element and makes the most
dreadful impression on the flesh. Hell is a place of
fire.

It is disputed among the learned what kind of
fire it is, and I wish we may never know. Augustine
and others affirm that it is material fire, but far hotter than any fire upon your hearts which is but
painted fire compared with this. I rather think that
the fire of the damned is partly material and partly
spiritual (which is the wrath of God to torment the
soul); that is the lake, the burning fire. Who knows
the power of God's anger! Who can dwell with these
burnings! It is intolerable to endure them and impossible to escape them.

(3) In hell there are chains of darkness.
Sinners who will not be bound by any law of God
shall have chains of darkness to bind them.

QUESTION: What should be the meaning of
that phrase, "chains of darkness"?

ANSWER: I suppose it may be this, to intimate
unto us that the wicked in hell shall not have power
to walk up and down, which perhaps might be a little easier, though very little, but they shall be
chained down fast so as not to stir. They shall be fas-
tened to that stake with chains of darkness. Oh, this
will be terrible indeed! Suppose a man should lie
always on a down bed and might not stir out of the
place—it would be very painful unto him. But to lie
as the damned upon the rack, always under the torturing scorching of God's wrath and to be tied and
not to move? How dreadful are the thoughts of this
condition of the wicked. They are under fire, darkness and chains.

To add to the torment of hell, there are two more things to show you that it shall be ill with the wicked, let them die when they will. The first is the worm. The second is the serpent.

First, there is the worm to torture the damned spirits; and this is no other but the worm of conscience in Mark 9:44: "where the worm never dieth." Oh, how dreadful it will be to have this worm!

Melanchthon calls the tormenting conscience a hellish fury. Conscience will be just as if a worm full of poison were feeding on the heart of a man. Those sinners who would never hear the voice of conscience shall feel the worm of conscience.

Second, as there is the worm to torment, so there is the devil, who is called "the old serpent." In hell, as there is the biting of the worm, so there is the stinging of the old serpent.

The damned shall be forced to behold the devil. I remember what Anselm said: "I would rather endure all the torments of this life than to see the devil with bodily eyes." But now this sight the wicked shall see whether they want to or not, and not only see, but feel the stinging of this old serpent the devil.

Satan is full of rage against mankind and will show no mercy. As he puts forth all his subtlety in tempting man, so he puts out all his cruelty in tormenting man. This is not all; there are two more things to set out the torments of hell.

These agonies and hell-convulsions shall be forever. Take Scripture for proof, Revelation 14:11: "And the smoke of their torment ascendeth forever and ever and they have not relief day nor night." Thus it is in hell. They would die but they cannot. The

wicked shall be always dying but never dead. The
smoke of the furnace ascends forever and ever. Oh,
who can endure thus to be ever upon the rack! This
word "ever" breaks the heart. Wicked men now
think the Sabbath is long: "When will the Sabbath
be over?" and they think a sermon and a prayer
long, but oh, how long will it be to lie in hell forever
and ever! After millions of years, their torments are
as far from ending as at the first hour they began.

Another aggravation of hell torment is that the
damned in hell have none to pity them. It is some
comfort, some ease to have our friends to pity us in
our sickness and want, but they have *no* friends.

Mercy will not pity them; mercy is turned into
fury. Christ will not pity them; He is no longer an
advocate for them. The angels will not pity them,
but will rejoice when they see the vengeance. They
exult and glory when they see the justice of God exe-
cuted upon His enemies. Oh, how sad this is to lie
in the scalding furnace of God's wrath and none to
pity them! When they cry out, God will laugh at
them. Hear this, all you who go on in sin. It will be
ill with the wicked. Therefore, turn from your sins
lest God tear you in pieces as a lion and there be
none to help you.

Application

USE 1. What a frightening word this is to all
wicked men who go on desperately to sin, to add
drunkenness to thirst. There has never been such
an inundation of wickedness as now. Men sin as if
they would spite God and dare Him to punish them.

Men sin so greedily as if they were afraid hell's gates would be shut up ere they got there. Oh, how manfully do many sin; they go to hell strongly in their wickedness! These are in a sad condition. It is sad at the hour of death and at the day of judgment. Wicked men live cursed and die damned. Sinners are the very mark that God will shoot at, His standing mark, and He never misses this mark. You know what the Scripture says, "There shall be weeping and gnashing of teeth." Latimer says, "That is sad fare where weeping is the first course and gnashing of teeth is the second course."

QUESTION. Whence is it that there is this gnashing of teeth?

ANSWER. First, it arises from the extremity of torment the wicked suffer. They are not able to bear it and know not how to avoid it.

Second, the wicked gnash their teeth in hell at the godly to see them in heaven, those whom they persecuted, scoffed, and jeered at, and themselves in hell. Luke 13:28: "When they shall see Abraham, Isaac, and Jacob, and all the prophets in the kingdom of God and they themselves shut out," they shall gnash their teeth at this. How may this amaze a wicked man! If all the curses in the Bible will make a man miserable, he shall be made so!

USE 2. Take heed that none of you here are found among the number of the wicked. Take heed of being of this black regiment that wears the devil's colors and fights under his banner. The sinner and the furnace shall never be parted. Take heed of those sins which will bring you to hellfire.

When you are tempted to any wickedness, think

to yourself, "How can I bear the fierceness of God's wrath forever? How can I lie in the winepress of God's wrath forever?" Take heed of those sins that will bring you into this place of torment.

I have read a story of a virgin who, being tempted by a young man to commit folly, said unto him, "Grant me but one request and I will do what you ask."

"What is that?" said he.

"Do but hold your finger one hour in this burning candle."

No, he would not do that.

Said she, "Will you not for my sake hold your finger an hour in the candle, and will you have my soul lie burning in hell forever?" Thus, she rebuked the temptation.

Does Satan tempt you to wickedness? Hold out this text as a shield to the devil to quench his fiery darts. Say this: "Oh, Satan, if I embrace your temptations, I must be under your tormenting to all eternity."

Therefore, labor to be righteous. It shall be well with the righteous. But take heed of sin. It shall be ill with the sinner.

I will conclude with a saying of Augustine: "When a man has been virtuous, the labor is gone but the pleasure remains. When a man has been wicked, the pleasure is gone but the sting remains."

Time's

Shortness

A sermon preached July 2, 1676, at the funeral of Mr.
John Wells, Late Pastor of Olave-Jury, London

Time's Shortness

"But this I say, brethren, the time is short."
1 Corinthians 7:29

The blessed Apostle in these words shows us what our station in the world is, and what all our secular enjoyments are. They are minute and transient. "But this I say, brethren, the time is short."

The text consists of two parts:

1. A kind compellation (or address): "Brethren."
2. A seasonable admonition: "The time is short."

1. A kind compellation: "Brethren." The saints of God are brethren. They are cemented together with the blood of Christ.

Then let there be no strife among them, seeing they are brethren (Genesis 13:8). Believers are regenerated by the same Spirit; they suck the same breasts, the promises, and wear the same garment, Christ's righteousness. They sit at the same board, the table of the Lord, and partake of the same glory, the inheritance in light (Colossians 1:12); and shall they not love? There ought to be no contending among God's people but as to who should love most.

Satan leaps at discord and warms himself at the fire of men's passions. If he cannot divide the spiritual members from their Head, he will endeavor to make them smite one against another. If he cannot

59

keep the saints from heaven, he will endeavor to
make them fall out by the way.

It was ill for Abraham's herdsmen and Lot's to
fall out when the Canaanite was in the land (Genesis 13:7). It is an ill time for mariners to be fighting
when the enemy is boring a hole in the bottom of
the ship. Take heed the popish enemy does not enter at your beaches.

Let Christians remember they are brethren.
Unity among brethren resembles the harmony
among angels. Psalm 133:1–3: "Behold, how good
and pleasant it is for brethren to dwell together in
unity. It is like the precious ointment upon the
head, as the dew of Hermon." It is compared to ointment because it is sweet, and compared to the dew of
Hermon because it makes everything fruitful. The
primitive Christians were of one heart (Acts 4:32).

Let us pray that that golden motto may be written
upon England: "One heart and one way" (Jeremiah
32:39). What a blessed place will heaven be where
our light shall be clear, our love shall be perfect,
and our joy shall be full.

2. A seasonable admonition: "The time is short."
This word "time" I shall take more strictly as the
term and period of man's life. The time is short.
The diverse instances of mortality may serve as so
many commentaries upon the text. The Greek word
for "short" alludes to mariners who roll up their
sails and bring them into a narrow compass when
the ship draws near the harbor. Though the sails of
man's life were spread larger in the times of the pa-
triarchs, now God is folding up these sails in a nar-
rower compass: "The time is short." The Scripture

frequently asserts the brevity and transitoriness of man's life. Psalm 89:47: "Remember how short my time is." Psalm 39:5: "Behold, Thou hast made my days as a hand-breadth," which is the least of the geometrical measures.

Job used three elegant metaphors to set forth the shortness of man's life. Job 9:25–26: "My days are swifter than a post; they are passed away as the swift ships, as the eagle that hasteth to her prey." If we look to the land, man's life is like a swift post. If we look to the sea, it is like a swift ship. If we look to the air, there it is like a flying eagle.

Life is compared to a cloud (Job 7:9). A cloud is a vapor drawn up by the sun into the middle region of the air. When this cloud comes to its full proportion, it is soon dispersed and blown away with the wind. Life gathers as a cloud, bigger and bigger, but all of a sudden it is dissipated by death. Our life is but a point to the globe, even less. Psalm 39:5: "My age is as nothing before Thee." There is but a span between the cradle and the grave. Solomon said, "There is a time to be born, and a time to die" (Ecclesiastes 3:2), but mentions no time of living, as if that were so short, it were not worth speaking of.

QUESTION. In what sense is the time of life short?

ANSWER. It is short in respect to the uncertainty; it may instantly expire. If a man who holds a farm at the will of his landlord is asked how long a time he has the farm, he will say no time at all because he is sure of none, as he may be turned out the next hour. So our time is short because of the uncertainty. Hezekiah, it is true, had a lease of fifteen years

sealed (Isaiah 38:5), but we have no such lease sealed
for us so death may be within a day's march.

There are so many casualties that it is a wonder if
the slender thread of our life is not cut off by un-
timely death. Have you not seen a virgin on the same
day dressed in her bride apparel and her winding
sheet?

Time is short in respect to its improvement. If we
reckon that for time which is well-spent, then time
is brought into a narrow compass indeed. A great
part of our time lies fallow. Take from our life all the
time of eating, drinking, sleeping, besides idle im-
pertinencies, and then how short is our time! How
little is the time wherein we can truly say, "This time
I have lived!" Oh, how little is the time which is
spent with God! Time misemployed is not time lived
but time lost.

Time is short compared with eternity. There is
no prospective glass to see to the end of eternity.
Eternity is a day that has no sun setting. It is a circle
without beginning or end. Eternity is a sum that can
never be numbered, a line that can never be mea-
sured. Reckon as many millions of years as there
have been minutes since the creation and they stand
as ciphers in eternity. The most elevated strains of
rhetoric cannot reach eternity. It is a sea without
bottom or banks. Time may be compared to a spot of
earth lying at the mouth of the great ocean. Time is
a spot on this side of eternity. What a little spot of
that is man's life! Thus you see, in this sense, time is
short.

It will not be long before the silver cord is loosed
and the golden bow broken (Ecclesiastes 12:6). By

"the silver cord," I understand the pith or marrow of the back which is called silver. This silver cord will soon be loosed. By "the golden bowl" is meant the membrane or skin wherein the brains are enclosed as in a bowl. This golden bowl will soon be broken. Time goes on apace. The poets painted time with wings because it flies so fast. In Joshua's days, when the sun and moon stood still, time went on. In Hezekiah's reign, when the sun went ten degrees backward, time went forward. Our whole life is nothing else but a passage to death where there is no staying by the way or slacking our pace.

USE 1. See what a poor inconsiderable thing life is. The time is short, and upon this small wire of time hangs the weight of eternity. Life is but a short scene acted here. It is but a vapor or puff of wind (James 4:14). Life is made up of a few flying minutes. Oh, then, how imprudent are those who will damn their souls to save their lives! He would be unwise who, to preserve a short lease, would lose his inheritance. How many there are who, to preserve this short life, will take indirect courses, defraud and oppress and build up an estate, but will pull down their souls! Many, to save their skins, will destroy their conscience. Spira, to preserve his life, abjured the faith.

The Irish make great reckoning of their skimeter (a warlike weapon), and will endure a blow on the arm to keep their skimeter from being hurt. I compare the soul to this skimeter. It is better to endure a blow on our body or estate than suffer our precious soul to be damaged. The soul is the man of the man. The soul of Plato is Plato. The soul is the

princely part, crowned with reason. It carries in it
some faint idea or resemblance of the Trinity. The
soul is a rich diamond set in clay. What folly it is to
save the clay and lose the diamond, like Tiberius the
emperor, who for a drink of water lost a kingdom!

USE 2. OF EXHORTATION.
BRANCH 1. Is time so curtailed and shortened?
Let us often contemplate the shortness of life.
Feathers swim upon the water but gold sinks into it.
Light, feathery spirits float in vanity, but serious
Christians sink deep into the thoughts of their sudden change. Deuteronomy 32:29: "Oh, that they were
wise, that they would consider their latter end."
Forgetfulness of the latter end makes life sinful and
death formidable. People naturally shrink back
from the thoughts of death. Amos 6:3: "They put far
away from them the evil day." When they are young,
they hope they shall spin out life to the blossoming
of the almond tree. When old age comes, they hope
to renew their strength as the eagle, though their
bodies are subject to corruption and they feel the
symptoms of mortality in them. Deafness of hearing
is death creeping in at the ear. Dimness of sight is
death creeping in at the eye. Yet they are so frantic
as to persuade themselves of long life. Bodily diseases are but death's harbingers which go before to
bespeak a lodging for death. Why, then, do men
dream of an earthly eternity? Psalm 49:11: "Their inward thought is that their houses shall continue
forever." Where is the man who contemplates time's
shortness, or makes another's death a looking glass
in which he may see his own dying face?

Some may say this discourse of the shortness of
time is fit for such as are consumptive, whom the
physicians have given over. But, for their parts, they
are well in health and may live many years.

Though your blood is fresh in your veins and
your bones are full of marrow, you know not how
short your time may be. He was not sick nor in fear
of sickness who said, "Soul, take thy ease," but that
night death terminated his lease (Luke 12:20).
Freshness of complexion is sometimes a lightning
before death. When the metal of which glass is
made begins to shine it is nearest melting. Persons
likely enough to live have been suddenly taken away
by convulsions and apoplexies. How soon may death
sound its alarm! It is reported of Zelenchus that the
first piece of household stuff he brought into
Babylon was a tombstone. Oh, meditate on the tran-
sience and brittleness of life! Think often of your
tombstone.

QUESTION. What advantage will accrue to us by
often thinking of our short stay here?

ANSWER 1. Meditation on the shortness of time
would cool the heat of our affections for the world.
These visible objects please the fancy, but they do
not so much delight us as delude us. They are suddenly gone from us. Worldly things are like a fair
picture drawn on the ice which the sun quickly
melts.

The time is short, so why should we love that over
much which we cannot keep over long? 1 Corinthians 7:31: "The fashion (or pageant) of the world pas-
seth away." Time passes away as a ship in full sail.
This, thought on seriously, would mortify covetous-

ness. Paul looked upon himself as ready to loose anchor and be gone. His love to the world had already died, Galatians 6:14: "The world is crucified to me and I unto the world." Who would covet that which has neither contentment nor continuance? Peter had the same view in 2 Peter 1:14: "Knowing that shortly I must put off this my tabernacle."

Among the Grecians, the city of Sparta had a king for a year and then he was to lay down his crown, which made everyone strive *not* to be king. Why should we so toil about the world as if we were to live here forever? What need is there for a long provision if it is for a short way? If we have enough to bear our charges to heaven, that should suffice. Suppose a man's lease were ready to expire and he should fall to building and planting; would not he be judged indiscreet? When our time is so very short now, to follow the world immoderately, as if we would fetch happiness out of the earth which God has cursed, is a degree of frenzy. We shall have no need of the earth soon but to be buried in it.

ANSWER 2. Meditation on the shortness of time should be a means to humble us. St. Augustine calls humility the mother of the graces. Balm sinks to the bottom of the water. A good Christian sinks low in humility, and what can sooner pull down the flags and banners of pride than to consider we are shortly dropping into the dust? The priest was to cast the feathers of the fowls by the place of the ashes (Leviticus 1:16). All your feathers of honor must shortly lie in the ashes. Shall not he who is clothed with mortality be clothed with humility? The thoughts of the grave would bury our pride. The Lord said to the

judges in Psalm 82:6, "I said you are gods"; but, lest
they should grow proud, He added a corrective, "but
you shall die like men." You are dying gods.
   ANSWER 3. Meditation on the shortness of time
would hasten our repentance. Repentance is as necessary as heaven. As radical moisture and natural
heat preserve life, so repenting tears and a heart
burning with love preserve the soul. It is natural to
delay repentance. We say with Haggai 1:2, "The time
is not yet come." But, the text says, the time is short.
Our life is a taper soon blown out.
   The thoughts of time's volubility and swiftness
would keep us from putting off our repentance. It is
no time for us to make a long work when God is
making a short work. It is observed of the birds of
Norway that they fly faster than the birds of other
countries. By the instinct of nature, knowing the
days in that climate to be very short, they therefore
make more haste to their nests. The consideration
of short abode here will make us avoid delays and fly
faster to heaven upon the wing of repentance.
   ANSWER 4. Meditation on the shortness of time
would give us an antidote against the temptations of
Satan. Temptation is Satan's eldest daughter who
woos for him. Satan does more mischief by his wiles
than his darts. He knows how to suit his temptation
as the husbandman knows what seed is proper for
such a soil. Satan tempted Achan with a wedge of
gold and David with beauty. It is hard to keep up the
banks of grace against the sea of temptation. I know
no better remedy against Satan's immodest solicita-
tions than this text: "the time is short."
   "What, Satan, do you tempt me to vanity when I

am going to give up my accounts? Shall I now be
sinning when tomorrow I may be dying? How shall I
look my judge in the face?" Christian, when Satan
sets sinful pleasure before you, show him a death's-
head. This will make temptations vanish.

ANSWER 5. The consideration of the shortness
of our stay in the world would be a help to temperance. It would make us sober and moderate in the
use of worldly comforts. By excess, we turn lawful
things into sin. The bee may suck a little honey
from the leaf, but put it into a barrel of honey and it
is drowned. We may with Jonathan dip the end of
the rod in honey, but not thrust it in too far. Noah
took too much of the grape (Genesis 9:21). The
flesh, when pampered, rebels. The best preservative
against intemperance is this: the time is short.

When we are feasting, death may quickly take
away the cloth. Plutarch reports that the Egyptians
used at their great banquets to bring in the image of
a dead man and say to their guests, "Look upon this
and proceed in your banquet." An excellent antidote
against a surfeit. Joseph of Arimathea erected a
sepulchre in his garden to spice his flowery delights
with the thoughts of death.

ANSWER 6. Meditation on the shortness of time
would much mitigate our grief for the loss of dear
relations. It is observable that when the Apostle said,
"The time is short," he immediately added. "Let
them that weep be as if they wept not."

No doubt the loss of relations is grievous to the
fleshly part. It is like pulling a limb from the body.
When God strikes us in our right eye, we weep. It is
lawful to give vent to our grief. Joseph wept over his

dead father. But though religion does not banish grief, it bounds it. We must weep as if we wept not. Rachel's sin was that she refused to be comforted (Matthew 2:18). It is thought that Origen died of grief. If anything can stop the issue of sorrow, at least assuage it, it is this, "The time is short." We shall shortly have our losses made up and enjoy our godly relations again in heaven.

ANSWER 7. Meditation on the shortness of time would make us highly value grace. Time is short, but grace is forever. 1 John 2:27: "The anointing which you have received of Him abideth in you." Grace is a blossom of eternity; it is an immortal seed (1 John 3:9). Grace is not blasted by death, but transplanted into a better soil. Grace is not a lease which soon expires, but an inheritance entailed forever. He who has true grace can no more lose it than the angels can who are fixed in their heavenly orb. Revelation 10:6, "The angel swore by Him that liveth forever that there should be time no longer." But grace shall survive time and run parallel with eternity.

BRANCH 2. If time is so short and winged, take heed of misspending this short time. To misspend time is the worse prodigality.

1. Take heed of spending time unprofitably. Domitian wasted much of his time in catching flies. Many live to cumber the ground. Judges 10:4: "Jair had thirty sons that rode on thirty ass-colts and they had thirty cities" and they died. So it may be said, such a one was born in the reign of such a king and he possessed such an estate and he died. His life was scarcely worth a prayer or his death worth a tear. An

idle person stands in the world but for a cipher, and God writes down no ciphers in the Book of Life. Many are like the wood of the vine—useless. Ezekiel 15:3: "Will men take a pin of it to hang any vessel thereon?" Too many resemble the lilies which toil not, neither do they spin. They spend their time as the emperor Caligula. He was at a great expense to provide a navy, and when it was provided he sent his mariners to sea to gather cockle-shells and so they sailed home again. God has furnished men with precious time wherein they may work out salvation, and they employ it vainly. They spin it out in impertinences. What reward can be expected when there is no work done? Who is crowned who never fights? Matthew 25:30: "Cast ye the unprofitable servant into utter darkness."

2. Take heed of spending time viciously. Many spend their short time in drinking, gaming, and whoring. Esau lost the blessing while he was hunting. Many lose heaven while they hunt after sinful pleasures. Sin is boiled to a great height in this age. Men study new oaths and count it a shame not to be impudent. They are steeped and parboiled in wickedness. They live in the world to infect others as the cockatrice with its breath poisons the herbs. What a dreadful account will they have to give who have nothing to show God but their treasons!

BRANCH 3. If the time of life is so short, let us improve it. Ephesians 5:16: "Redeeming the time." If a man had but a short time on a farm, he would make the best improvement of it and get as good a crop as he could out of it before he left it. The thoughts of our short stay here should make us improve this little inch of time.

That we may do this better, remember we must be accountable to God for time. God will say, "What have you done with your time?" If a lord entrusts his steward with money and goods, he expects that he should give him an account of what he has done with them and how he has employed them. All of us are stewards, and God will call us to a reckoning and say, "What have you done with the talent of time I entrusted you with?"

QUESTION: How should we improve this short time?

ANSWER: In general, mind salvation work (Philippians 2:12). He who lays up gold and silver is wise for his children, but he who gets salvation is wise for himself.

Especially, improve this short time by a serious examination. Christians, examine how the case stands between God and your souls. 2 Corinthians 13:5: "Prove yourselves." The Greek word is *dokimazete*: try yourselves as the goldsmith does his gold by a touchstone. Time is short, and what if God should say this night, "Give an account of your stewardship"?

Reckon with yourselves about your debts. Are your debts paid and your sins pardoned? Reckon with yourselves about making your will. Time is short; you may die before night. Have you made your will? I mean, in a spiritual sense, have you given up your will to God and, by solemn vow, set seal to the will? They are most fit to resign their souls to God who have resigned their wills to Him.

Call yourselves to account about your evidences.
Are your evidences for heaven ready? Your desires
are your evidences. Do you desire Christ for Himself
as beauty is loved for itself? Can nothing quench
your thirst but Christ's blood? Is your desire quick-
ened into endeavor? This is a blessed sign.

For want of this self-examination, many who are
well known to others are unknown to themselves.
They know not where they shall go when they die or
to what coast they shall sail—to hell or to heaven.

Improve this short time by laying hold of all the
seasons and opportunities for your souls. The
mariner takes the fit season; he sets to sea while the
wind blows. Time is short and opportunity (which is
the cream of time) is shorter. Let not the seasons of
mercy slip.

While God's Spirit strives with you, cherish His
sweet whispers and motions. When the dove came
flying to the windows of the ark, Noah reached out
his hand and pulled it into the ark. So when God's
Spirit (this blessed dove) comes to you, entertain
and welcome Him into the ark of your souls. If you
repulse the Spirit, He may refuse to strive any more.
Gospel seasons, though they are sweet, are swift.

While God's ministers are with you, make use of
them. Zechariah 1:5: "The prophets, do they live forever?" Their time (by reason of their labors) is
scarcely so long as others. We read of lamps within
the pitchers in Judges 7:16. Ministers are lamps, but
these lamps are in earthen pitchers which soon
break. Though ministers carry the word of life in
their mouths, yet they carry death in their faces.
Improve their labors while you have them. They

thirst for your happiness and, as so many bells, would chime in your souls to Christ.

Improve this short time by keeping up a close communion with God. 1 John 1:3: "Our communion is with the Father." This sweet communion with God is kept up by holy meditation. Genesis 24:63: "Isaac went out to meditate in the field at eventide." Meditation concocts divine truths in the mind. It brings God and the soul together. It is the bellows of the affections. It gives a sight and a taste of invisible glory. Psalm 104:34: "My meditation of Him shall be sweet."

Communion with God is kept up by prayer. Praying days are ascension days. Caligula placed his effigies in the capitol, whispering in Jupiter's ears. Prayer whispers in God's ears. It is a secret parley and conversation with God. On this mount of prayer, the soul has many sweet transfigurations.

Improve this short time by doing all the service you can for God. Wisdom may be learned from an enemy. Satan is more fierce because he knows his time is short (Revelation 12:12). We should act more vigorously for God seeing our time is short. Our lives should be as jewels—though little in quantity yet great in value. St. Paul knew his stay in the world was short, therefore, how zealous and active was he for God while he lived! 1 Corinthians 15:10: "I labored more abundantly than they all." Paul's obedience did not move as slowly as the sun on the dial, but as swift as the sun in the firmament. Is time short? Let us be "God-exalters." Let us bring glory to God in doing good to others. As aromatic trees sweat out their precious oils, so should we lay out our strength for the good of others.

Let us do good to their souls and convince the ignorant, strengthen the weak, and reduce the wandering. A good Christian is both a diamond and a lodestone—a diamond sparkling in sanctity and a lodestone for his attractive virtue in drawing others to Christ.

Let us do good to their bodies. Many at this day say to their sorrows, "You are our companions." Let our fingers drop with the myrrh of liberality. Hebrews 13:16: "to do good and communicate, forget not." Let us feed the hungry, clothe the naked, and be temporal saviors to others.

Could we thus improve our time, our lives, though short, would be sweet. This would be the way to cast abroad a fragrant, redolent smell in God's church, like the orange trees which perfume the air where they grow.

Could we thus improve our time, we might have our consciences drawing up a certificate for us, as in 2 Corinthians 1:12. Then it does not matter if the world censures as long as conscience acquits; it does not matter how cross the wheels go if the clock strikes rightly.

Could we thus improve our time, we might have an easy and joyful passage out of the world. This was Hezekiah's comfort when he thought he was lying on his deathbed. 2 Kings 20:3: "I beseech Thee, O Lord, remember how I have done that which is good in Thy sight." To improve time aright answers God's cost, credits religion, and saves the soul.

USE 3. Let this strike terror into every wicked

person who exhausts his strength in sin; his time is
short and then begins his hell. He spends his life in
a frolic. He takes the timbrel and harp and rejoices
at the sound of the organ (Job 21:12). But the time is
shortly coming when all his mirth shall cease.
Revelation 18:22, "The voice of the harpists, musi-
cians and trumpeters shall be heard no more at all
in thee." The grave buries all a sinner's joy. When a
wicked man dies, the devil gets a windfall.

Satan (in Samuel's shape) said to Saul, 1 Samuel
28:19, "Thou shall be with me tomorrow." The sinner has his lusts today and may be with the devil tomorrow. Who would envy the wicked their honor or
pleasure? They must pay dearly for it. They have a
short feast but a long reckoning. For a drop of
mirth, they must drink a sea of wrath; and who
knows the power of that wrath? Cardinal Bellarmine
said that if a man had a sight of hell it would be
enough to make an intemperate person sober.

Hell is the emphasis of torment. The sacrifice of
jealousy was to have no oil nor frankincense put to it
(Numbers 5:15). In hell, there is no oil of mercy put
to the torments of the wicked to assuage them, nor
is there any incense of prayer to appease God's
wrath. Oh, that sinners would in time break off their
iniquities! What has become of their intellect—have
they sinned away reason as well as conscience? The
time of life is short but the torments of hell are
lengthened out. Revelation 14:11: "The smoke of
their torment ascendeth up forever and ever."

USE 4. Here is a light side of the text to the
godly. They may be glad that their time here is

short; they cannot live but by dying. Behold, there is
honey at the end of the rod.

The time being short, their sinning time cannot
be long. Sin is a troublesome inmate. Romans 7:24
says that Paul, that bird of paradise, sighed and
groaned under corruption. A child of God mingles
sin with his duties. He cannot write a copy of holiness without blotting. There's a part of a regenerate
heart that sides with Satan. But be of good comfort,
the time is short. It is but for a short while,
Christians, that the dead man shall be tied to the living, that you shall be combatting a proud, unbelieving heart. The year of release is coming. Death does
to the godly as the angel did to Peter. It smites them
and makes their chains of sin fall off.

The time being short, their working time cannot
be long. In this life, much work is cut out. There is
the work of the hand, as the artificer works in his
trade (Proverbs 10:4). There is the work of the head.
Notions are the children of the brain, and there is
labor in bringing them forth. There is the work of
the heart, which is the hardest work—to search,
cleanse, and watch the heart. As a clock sometimes
goes faster, sometimes slower, so the heart sometimes goes faster in sin, sometimes slower in duty.
But here is the saint's comfort—their working time
is short. Revelation 14:13: "They rest from their
labors." When their bodies return to dust, their
souls return to rest.

The time being short, their suffering time cannot be long. Life is laden with trouble (Job 14:1).
You may as well separate weight from lead as trouble
from a man's life. We come into the world with a cry

and go out with a groan. Everyone has his yoke, and it is well if there is not a nail in it. Though the cross is heavy, we have but a little way to carry it. Death will give the godly a writ of ease. Job 3:17: "There (in the grave) the wicked cease from troubling."

The time being short, their waiting time cannot be long. The godly shall not be long out of heaven. While the blessed angels see the orient beauties that shine in God's face, believers live far from court, being imprisoned in the body. Here they rather desire God than enjoy Him. But the time is short, perhaps a few days or hours, and the saints shall be solacing themselves in the light of God's countenance. They shall leave their pillow of thorns and lay their head on Christ's bosom. Faith gives a propriety in God; death gives a possession. The wagons and chariots came rattling to old Jacob, but they were to carry him to his son, Joseph. Death's chariot wheels may come rattling to a believer, but it is to carry him home to his Father's house.

In that paradise of God, a Christian shall have more than he can think (Ephesians 3:20). He can think, "What if every mountain were a pearl, every flower a ruby, every sand in the sea a diamond, the whole globe a shining chrysolite?" But all his thoughts are too low and dwarflike to reach the glory of the celestial pyramids. The heavenly reward (as Augustine said) exceeds faith and, as the time is short, a Christian shall be in heaven before he is aware. Then he shall bathe his soul in those perfumed pleasures of paradise which run at God's right hand forevermore.

I am done with the text. Let me speak to the occasion. We are meeting here to commemorate the death of an eminent minister in this city, Mr. John Wells. I am sorry I am the actor in this mournful scene. But being requested by him in his life (in case I survived), I was willing to do this last office of love.

There has been a great mortality of ministers lately. The men of the world need not be so fierce against God's ministers; they will not trouble them long. God's taking away His ministers so fast (two in a day) bodes much evil. It presages the fall of a house when the pillars are removed.

Concerning this reverend brother deceased, it is not my purpose to use any hyperbolic encomiums or eulogies; only give me leave to strew a few flowers upon his hearse.

Our worthy friend was endued with learning and volubleness of speech. He could rightly divide the Word as a workman who needed not to be ashamed. He had seals to his ministry. Some of his hearers might call him their spiritual father.

Regarding his piety, he was not only a follower of that which was good, but a leader. He said not long before his death that he had brought this to an issue, that he loved God. He was fixed to his principles. Though he is by death a fallen star, he was not a wandering star.

His disposition was not morose but affable. He was a man of candor and courtesy. He obliged and won the affections of many to him. When grace and sweetness of nature meet it is like a pearl in a gold ring.

Regarding his preaching, he framed himself. He preached intelligibly to the capacity of his assembly of hearers because he was sure that a minister would never touch the hearts of his hearers if he shot over their heads. Ministers should be stars to give light, not clouds to darken the truth. Clearness is the grace of speech. Gregory Nazianzen preached plainly to the ignorant, yet was admired by the learned.

He was elaborate and painstaking in his work. Sloth in a minister is as bad as sleep in a sentinel. He would not offer that to God which cost him nothing. Christ bled for souls; well may we sweat. This good man, like a taper, wasted himself while he gave light to others.

He was a man of a forgiving spirit. He was not troubled with the overflowing of gall. Kindnesses he wrote in marble; injuries he forgot. He was very charitable. The backs and bellies of the poor were the furrows where he sowed the seeds of his liberality. But though his charity shone, he did not care that it might blaze. He is now taken from the evil to come.

For you who sat under his ministry, let me tell you that you have lost a friend and a guide. You have cause to be dear mourners. Let me request only this of you, that you would remember the many good instructions given you. Though he is dead, let not his sermons die, too, but labor to copy them in your lives.

The Fight

of Faith

Crowned

A sermon preached at the funeral of that
eminently holy man, Mr. Henry Stubs, 1678

Preface

Christian Reader,

It was not my intent to have this message appear publicly, but being requested by the near relations of this worthy deceased minister to print my sermon (which by their appointment was preached), I knew not well how to withstand their importunity. Indeed, I was more willing to let these lines be published that I might raise a pillar of remembrance to the precious name of Mr. Stubs.

The subject matter treated is the Christian's combat and crown. Oh, blessed crown which cannot be fully pencilled out in its orient colors, though an archangel should take the pencil! The Roman emperors had three crowns set upon their heads. The first was of iron, the second of silver, and the third of gold. God sets three crowns upon the elect: grace, joy, and glory. What should we thirst after but this incomprehensible bliss! If our thoughts dwelt above, we would live sweeter lives. The higher the lark flies, the sweeter it sings.

Cyprus was anciently called Macaria, the blessed island, but it is more true that heaven is the blessed island. It is a place where sorrow cannot live and joy cannot die. It may be compared to the fields of Sicily where there is continual spring and flowers all the year long. Could our meditations mount up to the empyrean delights, how would the world disappear and shrink into nothing! To those who stand upon the top of the Alps, the great cities of Campania seem as little villages. After St. Paul was wrapped up into the third heaven, the world was crucified to him (Galatians 6:14). When worldly things are in their highest meridian of glory, they hasten to a sunset. Let us live more in the altitudes and take a prospect of the eternal recompenses. What can be more delicious or sacred than to have Christ in our heart and the crown in our eye?

I have inserted something more into this sermon than straits of time would permit in the delivery. If it kindles holy ardors in the breasts of any and quickens their pace in the way to heaven, I have my wish. That this may be effected is the prayer of him who is:

Thy friend and servant in the gospel,

Thomas Watson

The Fight of Faith Crowned

"I have fought a good fight, I have finished
my course, I have kept the faith; henceforth
is laid up for me a crown of righteousness."
2 Timothy 4:7–8

These words were spoken by Paul, the aged, not
long before his death. Verse 6 says, "I am now ready
to be offered," or, as the Greek word signifies, "to
have my blood poured out in sacrifice." What a comfort it was to make this noble declaration before his
departure: "I have fought a good fight." The text falls
into three parts:

1. **Paul's courage:** "I have fought a good fight."
2. **Paul's constancy:** "I have finished my course, I
   have kept the faith."
3. **Paul's crown:** "Henceforth is laid up for me a
   crown of righteousness."

Here is a large field and I can but pluck a few
ears of corn. I begin with the first part of the text.

1. Paul's courage: "I have fought a good fight. I
have fought to an agony." Observe, first, that a Christian's life is military. 1 Timothy 1:18 says, "That thou
mayest war a good warfare." A saint's life is not ef-
feminate and slothful, but like the soldier's life:

(1) *In respect to hardship.* A soldier does not have his soft bed or daily fare but undergoes tedious marches; and such is the Christian life. 2 Timothy 2:3 says, "Thou, therefore, endure hardness as a good soldier of Jesus Christ." We must not be delicate (as Tertullian speaks), silken Christians, but expect to wrestle with difficulties. The naked neck is too soft and tender to bear the cross of Christ.

(2) *In respect to watchfulness.* A soldier gets up to his watchtower and sends abroad his scouts for fear the enemy may surprise him. A Christian must stand sentinel and be ever on his guard. It was Christ's watchword, Mark 13:37, "I say to you all, watch." When you have prayed against sin, watch against temptation.

(3) *In respect to combat.* 1 Timothy 6:12: "Fight the good fight of faith." In order to fight, a Christian must get his armor and weapons ready.

He must get his armor ready. The care of most is to get riches, not armor. There are two things absolutely needful—food and armor. It is necessary to get Christ for our food and grace for our armor, without which there is no abiding the day of trial. A soldier who wears his prince's colors but has no armor will soon flee the field. In a procession, if you wear Christ's colors but have not the armor of God upon them, you will turn your backs in the day of battle.

There are two chief pieces of the spiritual armor. First, the helmet is divine hope. 1 Thessalonians 5:8: "For a helmet the hope of salvation." A helmet is to defend the head so that it is not hurt. So the hope of salvation as a helmet defends a person and makes him lift up his head in the greatest dangers. Christians, be sure you get the right helmet, because the helmet of hope may be counterfeited.

The first deceit of the helmet, or a false hope, is dead hope. Hypocrites have a faint will. They hope for heaven, but exert no activity in working out salvation. True hope is a "lively hope" (1 Peter 1:3). Hope of glory sets an edge upon the affectations and adds wings to the endeavor.

A false hope is an unclean hope. A man hopes, but sins. It is vain to speak of hopes of salvation and have the marks of damnation. True hope is a helmet made of pure metal. 1 John 3:3: "He who has this hope purifieth himself."

A false hope is vanishing. It is not a helmet but a spider's web. The least terror of conscience makes it vanish, but a true hope is permanent. Proverbs 14:32: "The righteous hath hope in his death." In a dying hour, his hope is in a living God.

Quintian the persecutor commanded one of his men to cut off the breasts of Agatha, a martyr.

"Do your worst, tyrant," said the martyr, "yet I have two breasts which you cannot touch. The one is of faith, the other of hope." Oh, get the right helmet! The devil laughs at hypocrites who are deceived with false armor. A fool is content with a paper helmet.

The second piece of the spiritual armor is the breastplate, which is love. "Putting on the breastplate of love" (1 Thessalonians 5:8). This breastplate is inseparable; it may be shot at but it cannot be shot through, Song of Solomon 8:7. A soul armed with love will go through a sea and a wilderness and will die in God's service.

A Christian must get his weapons ready. Ephesians 6:16: "Above all things taking the shield of
faith."

Epaminondas was not as careful of his life as of
his shield. A shield is of great use. It defends the
head, it guards the vital organs, and it keeps the arrow from entering into the body. The shield of faith
defends the heart and beats back the fiery darts of
temptation. A Roman soldier resisted Pompeii's
army until he had over a hundred darts sticking in
his shield. Hold forth the shield of faith and nothing can hurt you.

Ephesians 6:17: "The sword of the Spirit which is
the Word of God." It is good for a soldier to be well
skilled in his weapon. The Word of God is a weapon
to stab lust at the heart. It is observable that when
the devil tempted our Savior he ran to Scripture and
said "It is written" three times. Christ wounded the
old serpent with this spiritual weapon.

Having gotten into this warlike posture, a
Christian must enter the arena and fight the good
fight of faith. In the future life, the saints shall be
out of the noise of the drum and cannon, and not
one stroke shall be struck more. Then they shall not
appear in their armor, but in their white robes and
with palm branches in their hands in token of victory. Here they must fight the Lord's battles, and
have no cessation of arms until death. And there is a
threefold regiment they must encounter:

The first regiment is the lusts of the flesh war
against their souls (1 Peter 2:11). The flesh is a sly
internal enemy and least suspected. An enemy
within the walls of the castle is most dangerous.

Luther said he feared his own heart more than Pope or Cardinal. The heart is the fomenter of sin. It mints evil thoughts and blows up the coals of fiery passions. It is the Trojan horse out of which comes a whole army of lusts. Shall we not fight the good fight and discharge with the fire of zeal against this bosom traitor, the flesh? The primitive Christians chose rather to be destroyed by lions without than by lusts within.

The second regiment to be resisted is Satan and the infernal powers. 1 Peter 5:8: "Your adversary the devil as a roaring lion walks about." He walks about not as a pilgrim, but a spy who narrowly observes. There were persons lying in wait for Samson (Judges 16:12). Satan, like a musketeer, lies in a bush, and his design carries death in the front, "seeking whom he may devour." He tempts one man to be drunk, another to be unclean. He sets kingdoms quarreling that at last he may devour them, like the person who sets two gamecocks to fight, so that once they have killed each other he may sup with their carcasses. Does this hellish Goliath come into the field and defy the living God? Shall not some spear be lifted up against him? 1 Peter 5:9: "Whom resist steadfast in faith."

The third regiment Christians must fight against is the enchantments of the world. The world is a flattering enemy. It kills with embracing. Worldly things hinder our passage to the holy land. They choke good affections like the earth puts out the fire. Whom the world kisses, it betrays. Heliogabalus made ponds of sweet water to drown himself and gilded poisons to poison himself. The world de-

stroys millions with her sweet waters of pleasure and
her gilded poisons of preferment. Let us then gird
on our armor and fight valorously.

For good reason we should fight the fight of
faith, because we carry rich treasure about us. He
who carries a charge of money about him should be
in a fighting posture. We carry a precious soul about
us. If the cabinet of the body is so curiously wrought
and embellished (Psalm 139:15), then what is the
jewel in it? The soul is a spark and beam of celestial
brightness, a blossom of eternity; and shall not we,
by our martial prowess and chivalry, defend this
treasure? To be robbed of the soul is an irreparable
loss. God (said Chrysostom) has given you two eyes.
If you lose one, you have another; but you have only
one soul and if you are robbed of that, you are undone forever.

USE. Is the Christian life military? To blame,
then, are they who have no spiritual artillery, nor do
they make one ally against the enemy. It is death to
go abroad unarmed. People spend time in dressing
themselves by the glass and putting on their jewels,
but do not put on their sacred armor. They take the
timbrel and harp and rejoice at the sound of the organ, as if they were rather in music than in battle.
Lycurgus would have no man's name written upon
his tomb but he who died manfully in war. God
writes no man's name in the Book of Life but he
who dies fighting the good fight of faith.

Give battle to sin and Satan, and pursue them
with a holy malice. To encourage you in the fight,
let these things be weighed:

1. It is a good fight. It is a lawful war. Princes may commence a war to invade other men's rights and properties, but God has proclaimed war against sin. Colossians 3:5: "Mortify, therefore, your members . . . fornication, inordinate affection."

2. We have a good captain. Jesus Christ is the Captain of our salvation (Hebrews 2:10). If a flock of sheep has a lion for their captain, they need not fear the wolf. Christ is the Lion of the tribe of Judah (Revelation 5:5). He not only leads us on in our march, but helps us in the fight. A captain may give his soldier armor, but he cannot give him strength. Christ animates and strengthens us (Isaiah 41:10). He puts His spirit within us, and so we are more than conquerors (Romans 8:37).

3. Our enemy, Satan, is beaten in part already. Christ has given him his death's-wound upon the cross (Colossians 2:15). The devil may roar against a child of God, but shall not hurt him. He could not touch Job's life, much less his soul; therefore, fear not. "Resist the devil and he will flee from you" (James 4:7). Satan is a conquered enemy. He knows no march but running away.

4. Fighting is the best way to have peace. By sitting still, we tempt the enemy to fall upon us and wound us. Our peace is preserved by war with Satan. He who has been skirmishing all day may take David's pillow at night and say, "I will lay me down in peace."

QUESTION. How may we fight the good fight so as to overcome?

ANSWER. Let us fight in the strength of Christ. Philippians 4:13: "I can do all things through Christ

who strengtheneth me." Grace itself, if it has not a
good second, will be beaten out of the field. Some
fight against sin in the strength of their vows and
resolutions, and so are foiled. We must go out
against our spiritual antagonists in the strength of
Christ like David went out against Goliath in the
name of the Lord (1 Samuel 17:45). "The saints over-
came the accuser of the brethren by the blood of the
Lamb" in Revelation 12:11.

We must fight on our knees by prayer. Prayer
whips the devil. The arrow of prayer, put into the
bow of the promise and shot with the hand of faith,
pierces the old serpent. Prayer brings God over to
our side, and then we are on the strongest side. Let
us pray that God will enable us to overcome all our
ghostly enemies. While Joshua was fighting, Moses
was praying on the mount (Exodus 17:11). So while
we are fighting, let us be praying (Ephesians 6:13–
18). The way to overcome is upon our knees.

2. Paul's constancy: "I have finished my course, I
have kept the faith." It is as if Paul should say, "I have
finished my course. I have run out nature's lease. I
have come to the period of life prefixed and am step-
ping into eternity. I have kept the faith, that is, I
have kept the doctrine of faith. I have lived the life
of faith."

Observe, Christians should hold on till they
come to the finishing of their faith. It is not enough
to begin well, to put forth fair blossoms of religion
at first, but we must continue firm to the end. This is
the glory of a Christian—not only to hold forth the
truth, but to hold fast the truth. It is a beautiful sight

to see silver hairs crowned with golden virtues. It was
the honor of the church of Thyatira that her last
works were better than her first (Revelation 2:19).
The excellency of a medicine is when it keeps its
virtue. To finish the course and keep the faith is to
be like generous wine that keeps its spirits to the
last drawing.

USE 1. Here is a bill of indictment against those
who, before the finishing of their course, have departed from the faith. They are fallen to worldliness
or wantonness; the very mantle of their profession is
fallen off. Judas has many successors. Demas forsook
God, and afterwards became a priest in an idol temple, said Dorotheus. Julian bathed himself in the
blood of beasts offered in sacrifice to heathen gods,
and so, as much as in him lay, washed off his bap-
tism. Things which move from an artificial spring
quickly cease. Profane hearts, having only external
artifices of piety, but lacking a vital principle of
grace, soon make a stop in religion. How can they
adhere to God who never loved Him? The soldier
who has no true love for his commander will throw
off his colors. Hosea 8:3: "Israel has cast off the
thing that is good." We have had more shipwrecks at
land than at sea. Men shipwreck their conscience
(1 Timothy 1:19). Apostates unravel the work they
have been doing for heaven. They pick out all their
golden stitches. As if a painter should with a pencil
draw a curious piece and then come with his sponge
and wipe it out again. Apostates drop as windfalls
into the devil's mouth, having disparaged the ways
of God and put Christ to open shame (Hebrews 6:6).
God will make them do penance in hell.

USE 2. Persevere in the faith. What is a man the
better to run some part of the race and then tire, to
come within an inch of heaven and then fall short?
Who makes reckoning of corn that sheds before
harvest, or fruit that falls from the tree before it is
ripe. Oh, Christians, remember your salvation is
now nearer (Romans 13:11)! You are within prospect
of the holy land and will you now tire in your
march? This is as if a ship laden with jewels and
spices, within sight of the shore, should be cast
away. Or it is as if a Jew had run to the city of refuge
and had gotten within half a furlong of the city and
then fainted and been slain by the avenger of blood.
It was Beza's prayer, "Lord, perfect that which Thou
hast begun in me that I may not suffer shipwreck
when I am almost in the haven."

Consider that persevering in the faith is a note of
discrimination between a true saint and a hypocrite.
The hypocrite sets up the trade of religion, but will
soon break. He advances his mast and topsail and
sets out for heaven, but in time and temptation falls
away (Matthew 13:21). But a true Christian is fixed in
holiness. He is not as a wave of the sea, but as a rock
in the sea. His zeal, like the fire of the vestal virgins
in Rome, is always kept burning.

That we may spin out this fine thread of religion
to its full length and hold out to the end:

1. Let us be well grounded in the fundamentals
of religion (Colossians 1:23)—the doctrine of justification, regeneration, resurrection and eternal recompenses. Such as are unprincipled will be led into
any error, the Mass or the Koran. You may lead a
blind man anywhere and he will hardly ever suffer

for the truth if he does not know it.

2. If we would hold on in the faith, let us preserve a jealous fear of ourselves. Fear is the soul's safeguard. It causes vigilance and banishes presumptions. Romans 11:20: "Be not high-minded but fear." If God lets go His maintenance we fall. How many have been overturned with self-confidence as the vessel with the sail. Pendleton's proud bragging was soon confuted. Instead of his fat melting in the fire, his heart melted. The fear of falling keeps us from falling. Fear begets prayer, prayer begets strength and strength begets constancy.

3. If we would keep the faith to the end, let us labor to taste the sweetness of religion in our own souls. Psalms 34:8: "Oh, taste and see that the Lord is good." The light of truth is one thing; the relish is another. Psalm 119:103: "How sweet are Thy words unto my taste, yea sweeter than honey." Many fall away because they never tasted what religion was. They could taste some sweetness in corn and oil, but its promises were dry breasts. If the wine of the Word has ever cheered our heart, we will never part with it.

4. If we would continue our progress in the ways of God, let us be inlaid with sincerity. This silver thread must run through the whole chain of our duties. A Christian may have a double principle, but he does not have a double heart. He is perfect with the Lord (Deuteronomy 18:13). Nothing will hold out but sincerity. Psalm 25:21: "Let integrity preserve me." When Job could not hold fast his estate, he held fast his religion. How was this? From his sincerity. Job 27:6: "My righteousness I hold fast and will not let it go; my heart shall not reproach me so

long as I live." The garment of Job's profession did
not tear because it was lined with sincerity.

3. Paul's crown. The third part of the text is Paul's
crown: "Henceforth is laid up for me a crown of
righteousness." It is a crown laid up. A Christian's
best things are to come. Well might the Apostle say,
"It doth not yet appear what we shall be" (1 John
3:2). We are here as princes in disguise. The world
knows us not, but there is a crown laid up for us.
While we are laying *out* for God, He is laying *up* for
us.

What crown is this? A crown of righteousness.
The felicity of heaven is described sometimes by a
city of riches (Hebrews 11:10), sometimes by a country of pleasure (Hebrews 11:16), sometimes by a
crown of honor. This crown has various appellations:

It is called a crown of glory (1 Peter 5:4). It is full of
splendor, therefore it is said to be bespangled with
stars (Revelation 12:1). We can no more bear a sight
of this crown until God enlarges our capacities than
a weak eye can bear the dazzling beams of the sun.

It is called a crown of life (James 1:12). Whoever
heard before of a living crown? It is a crown of life,
not only (as Grotius said) because it is bestowed in
the life to come, but because it enlivens with joy. It
not only crowns the head but cheers the heart. It is a
living crown.

It is called a crown of righteousness in the text,
not that it is rightly due us or comes of merit as the
papists corruptly gloss. We cannot deserve a crumb
at God's hands, much less a crown. That which mer-

its must be a gift, not a debt. Whatever service we do for God is a due debt; nay, we cannot pay it; nay, that which we pay is not in current money; our duties are stained with sin. Where then is merit? It is called a crown of righteousness because it is purchased by Christ's righteousness, and because it is righteous for God, having promised this crown, to bestow it.

Hence, for the persevering saint, there is laid up a crown of righteousness in heaven. A crown is the highest ensign of worldly happiness. It is only for kings and persons of renown to wear. There is a crown of righteousness laid up for the elect. It is a weighty crown. The Hebrew word for glory signifies a weight, things that are precious. The more weighty they are, the more they are worth. The weightier a chain of pearl is the more it is worth. The heavenly crown is expressed by a weight of glory in 2 Corinthians 4:17. This crown of righteousness exceeds all earthly crowns.

It is more refined. Earthly crowns are interwoven with troubles. They are not made without crosses. It was King Henry VII's motto: "A crown of gold hung in a bush of thorns." But the saint's crown is not mixed with care. It adds no sorrow with it.

The crown of righteousness is given to every individual saint. Here the crown goes but to one person; a crown of gold will fit but one head. But in heaven, every saint is a king and has his crown.

The crown of righteousness does not draw envy to it. David's crown was an eyesore to Absalom, and he would have plucked it from his father's head. In the life to come different degrees of glory shall neither stir up pride nor cause envy, for though one

crown may be bigger than another, everyone's
crown shall be as big as they can carry.

The crown of righteousness is everlasting. What
disparages earthly crowns is that they are corruptible. Proverbs 27:24: "Doth the crown endure to every
generation?" Terrestrial crowns soon smolder into
the dust, but the crown of righteousness is a crown
of immortality; it neither spends nor fades. 1 Peter
5:4: "Ye shall receive a crown of righteousness which
fadeth not away." Eternity is a jewel of the saint's
crown.

QUESTION: What is the matter of which the celestial crown is made?

ANSWER: The crown itself consists in the beautiful sight and fruition of the all-glorious God. What
else is the angel's crown but the beholding of God's
face (Matthew 18:10)? To experience transforming
sights of God will ravish the elect with infinite delight. Chrysostom said, "The souls of the blessed
shall be bespangled with some of those illustrious
beams of God's glory which shall be transparent
through the bright mirror of Christ's human nature."

If there was such gladness when Solomon was
crowned (1 Kings 1:40): "They rejoiced with great
joy, so that the earth rent with the sound", what
mighty acclamations and triumphs will be on the
saints' coronation day? Such will be the ecstasies
and divine raptures of joy as exceed our very faith.
The delights of heaven may be better felt than expressed. Whatever can be said of the celestial crown
is but as a drop in relation to the ocean, nay,
scarcely so much.

QUESTION: When shall the saints receive this crown of righteousness?

ANSWER: They shall receive it in part immediately after death. Before their bodies are buried, their souls are crowned. 2 Corinthians 5:8: "Absent from the body, present with the Lord." If the crown were not instantly bestowed after death, it would be better for believers to stay here for they are daily increasing their grace. Here they have some bunches of grapes by the way, sweet foretastes of God's love. So they had better stay here if they do not have a speedy transition and passage to glory. But this is the consolation of believers, that they shall not stay long for their preferment. No sooner did Lazarus die than he had a convoy of angels to carry him to Abraham's bosom. Christians, you may be happy before you are aware; it is but winking and you shall see God.

The full coronation will be at the resurrection when the bodies and souls of believers shall be reunited. Their bodies shall be crowned with immense felicity and clarified like Christ's glorious body.

QUESTION: But why is the crown deferred at all? Why is it not set on a Christian's head presently?

ANSWER: It is not yet the proper season. We are heirs under age. We receive but the first fruits of the spirit (Romans 8:23). Grace is in its minority now, though some princes have been crowned in their cradle, God crowns none till they are of perfect stature. Sin incorporates with grace. Would we partake of glory while we partake of sin?

Our work is not yet done; we have not finished

the race. The laborer does not receive his pay until
his work is done. Christ's reward was deferred until
He had perfected His work. John 17:4–5: "I have finished the work which Thou gavest Me to do and
now, O Father, glorify Me." The Lord does not think
we should have our pay beforehand. When we have
arrived at the end of our faith, then comes salvation
(1 Peter 1:9).

Then there is nothing lost by solid piety. After
fighting the good fight of faith comes the crown of
righteousness. When we hear of the severe part of
religion, steeping our souls in the briny tears of repentance, mortifying our complexion of sin, we are
ready to grumble and mutiny; but do we serve God
for nothing? Will He not compensate our labors
with a crown, yes, a crown which far exceeds our
thoughts as it does our deserts? No man can say
without wrong done to God that He is a hard master.
The Lord gives double pay. He gives great rewards in
His service here—inward joy and peace—and afterwards He refreshes us with the delights of paradise
which are without intermission and expiration. Oh,
what a vast difference there is between duty enjoyed
and glory prepared! What is the shedding of a tear
to a crown?

See what contrary ways the godly and the wicked
go at death. The godly are advanced to crowns of
glory; the wicked are bound with chains of darkness
(Jude 6). But what are these chains? Surely such as
no strong liquid can eat asunder. By these chains, I
understand God's sovereign omnipotence, fasten-
ing sinners under wrath (as the chain does the pris-
oners) so that they cannot stir. Sinners may break

the chain of God's precepts but they cannot break the chain of His power. This is the unparalleled misery of impenitent souls: they do not go to a crown when they die but to a prison. Oh, think what horror and despair will possess the wicked when they see themselves engulfed in tremendous flames and their condition is hopeless, helpless, and endless!

A servant under the old law who had a hard master yet, every seventh year being a year of Jubilee or release, might go free. But in hell there is no year of release when the damned shall go free (Mark 9:44). What is to become of men's intellect? Have they lost their reason as well as their conscience? Why do they not think to themselves what sin in time will bring them to. Though now it shows its color in the glass, yet in the end it will bite as a serpent (Proverbs 23:32). If a man had but a sight of hell (said Bellarmine) it would be enough to make him sober and live a most mortified life.

See the grand folly of those who for vain pleasures and profits will lose this celestial crown. It may be said of them, as in Ecclesiastes 9:3, "Madness is in their heart." Tiberias, for a drink of water, lost his empire. Men swallow temptations like pills which grip their consciences and afterwards make them forfeit blessedness. This will accent and enhance a sinner's torment, and will cause gnashing of teeth, to think how sillily he lost paradise. For a flash of impure joy, he parted with the quintessence of happiness. Would it not vex one to think he should be so seduced as to part with his land of inheritance for a bit of music? Such are they who let heaven go for a song. If Satan could make good his boast in giving all the glory and kingdoms of the world, they could not countervail the loss of heaven's crown. When a sinner dies, the devil abandons him as a fool.

If the saints are installed and have the royal crown set upon them at death, then what little cause have we to mourn immoderately at the death of godly friends! God allows us tears. Jacob wept over his dead father. Tears give vent to grief, but there is no reason why we should grieve excessively for our pious friends. They receive a crown; and shall we mourn when they have preferment? Suppose you had a dear relation beyond the sea and you heard he was crowned king. Would you grieve to hear of his advancement? The friend who dies in the Lord receives immediately a crown of righteousness, and will you be cast down with sorrow? Why should you shed tears immoderately for those who have all tears wiped from their eyes? Why should you be swallowed up in grief for those who are swallowed up in joy? They are removed hence for their advantage, as if one should be removed out of a smoky cottage to a palace.

The prophet Elijah was removed in a fiery chariot to heaven. Shall Elisha weep inordinately because he enjoys not the company of Elijah? Is it not better to have sparkling crowns and white robes than to sojourn in the tents of Kedar? Is it not better to live among angels than fiery serpents? Is it not best to have Christ's banner of love displayed over us? Are there any sweeter smiles or softer embraces than His? Why then should any bathe and even entomb themselves in sorrow for their relations?

Theocritus says it was a custom among the ancients to have the funeral banquet because of the felicity they supposed the deceased parties entered into. Oh, you who hang your harp upon the willows and, with Rachel, refuse to be comforted! Remember there is no wiping away tears from the eye but with the winding sheet. Your friend could not be in the region of the blessed till he died. His dying day was his ascension day. Oh, then, keep your tears for your sins, but do not torment yourself with grief for him whose soul is as holy as it would be and as happy as it can be.

Are we heirs to this glorious crown? Such only as are righteous persons shall wear the crown of righteousness. The work of righteousness goes before the crown of righteousness (Isaiah 32:17). Are we not only morally but theologically righteous? Have we a righteousness of imputation procured for us by Christ's merit, and a righteousness of implantation produced in us by His Spirit? Are we consecrated with the anointing oil of grace? God gilds the elect with the beams of His own holiness and makes them shine like Himself. Have we both circumcision of heart and circumspection of life? If we are righteous persons, we are sure to wear the crown of righteousness.

Let not the profane presume happiness. Let them not think to go to heaven leaping out of Delilah's lap into Abraham's bosom. 1 Corinthians 6:9: "Know ye not that the unrighteous shall not inherit the kingdom of God?" God will not lay a viper in his bosom or set a crown upon the head of a swinish sinner.

USE OF EXHORTATION.

1. It has a double aspect to all in general. Believe that there is a crown of righteousness laid up for all who fight the good fight. Some of the rabbis said that the great dispute between Cain and Abel was about the world to come. Abel affirmed a crown of recompense for the godly; Cain denied it. This truth should be graven upon our hearts as with the point of a diamond. Carnal persons look upon the felicities of the other world as a platonic idea or fancy. They do not see the crown with bodily eyes; therefore they question it. The verity of the soul may as well be questioned because, being a spirit, it cannot be seen. Doubting principles is the next step toward denying them. Let us set our seal to this: There is a crown of righteousness laid up. Where should your faith rest but upon a divine testimony? The whole earth hangs upon the word of God's power, and shall not our faith hang upon the word of His promise? Titus 1:2: "In hope of eternal life which God who cannot lie hath promised."

The saint's crown is purchased by Christ's blood (Ephesians 1:14), and Christ will not lose His purchase. What was the end of Christ's ascension? He went up to heaven not only to invest Himself, but all believers, with glory, as a husband takes up land in another country on behalf of his wife. What did Christ pray for but that all the saints might be with Him (John 17:24)? What Christ prayed for as a man, He has power to give us since He is God. Besides, the Lord has given us the unction of His Spirit to prepare us, and the earnest of His Spirit to assure us of happiness (2 Corinthians 1:21). He will not lose His earnest so that the crown of righteousness shall indubitably be bestowed. To question this is to destroy the main article of our creed which is life everlasting. Such atheists who judge the eternal recompenses to be fictions put God to swear against them that they shall never see life.

Strive for this crown. I have read of those who travel in long pilgrimages to the Holy Land. They have hard lodgings and pass through a number of dangers, and at the end of their journey pay a large tribute at the Pisan Castle to the Turks. When they come there, they see only a bare sepulchre where it is supposed their Savior lay. Did they take such pains to gratify their superstitious devotion? What herculean labor, then, should a Christian undertake in his journey to the true land of promise, whereby he shall both see and enjoy his Savior, and not enter into His sepulchre but His palace and be eternally crowned with the delights of the Jerusalem above?

If we would take as many pains for heaven as others do for the world, undoubtedly we might obtain it, reaching forth unto those things which are ahead (Philippians 3:13)—a metaphor taken from racers who reach their neck forward and strain every limb to lay hold upon the prize.

There are two things requisite for a Christian—a watchful eye and a working hand. To achieve our purpose, let us add pursuit. What scuffling is there for outward honors? Men will wade through blood for a crown. Was there such strife for a corruptible crown in the Olympian races? Sometimes the crown bestowed upon the victor was made of olive, sometimes of myrtle, sometimes of cinnamon enclosed

in gold, but still it was corruptible. Oh, then, how
strenuously should we labor for the garland made of
the flowers of paradise which never fade! With what
vigor and resolution did Hannibal march over the
Alps for the obtaining of terrestrial kingdoms! How
should we act then with extreme intensity for that
orient crown which shines ten thousand times
brighter than the sun in its meridian splendor.

Luther spent three hours a day in prayer. Anna,
the prophetess, departed not from the temple, but
served God with fasting and prayers night and day
(Luke 2:37). The learned Calvin, Jewell, and Perkins
were indefatigable in their pursuit after glory.

Let us look to this cloud of witnesses and, turn-
ing back to ourselves, ply our oar and double our ef-
forts. Who would not toil all day to catch salvation at
night? When the flesh cries out, what weariness is
it? Who can endure all this labor? It is worse endur-
ing hell. The labor for heaven, though it seems
pungent, is transient. The fight is quickly over and
then comes the unfading crown.

2. It has a particular aspect to believers. Be full of
pantings and longings for this crown of righteousness. Does not the banished prince desire his native
country? The unwillingness of Christians to go
hence shows:

(1) *The weakness of their faith.* They question
their interest in this excellent glory. Were their title
to heaven more cleared, they would need patience to
be content to stay here any longer.

(2) *The weakness of their love.* Love (as Aristotle
said) desires union. If men loved Christ as they
should, they would desire to be united to Him in

glory. Paul desired to be dissolved and be with Christ (Philippians 1:23). It was the speech of a holy man on his deathbed, "My heart is in heaven, Lord; lead me to that glory which I have seen already as through a glass."

We are encompassed with a body of sin. Should we not long to shake off this viper? We are combatting with Satan. Should we not be willing to be called out of the bloody field, where the bullets of temptation fly so fast, that we may receive a victorious garland? We now live far from court. We would rather desire God than enjoy Him. Should we not long to be crowned with the blissful sight of God's face?

Though we should be content to stay here to do God's service, we should ambitiously desire to be always sunning ourselves in the light of God's countenance. Think what it will be to be led into Christ's wine cellar, to have the kisses of His mouth, to smell the savor of His ointments, to lie in His bosom, that bed of love. Think what it will be like to have unstained honor, unparalleled beauty, and unmixed joy. What will it be like to tread upon stars, to dwell among cherubim, and to feast on those heavenly delicacies and rarities wherewith God Himself is delighted? I think our souls should be big with longing for these things, and we should be put into such a blessed pathos of desire as Monica, who, hearing of the joys of heaven, cried out, "What should I do here? Why is my soul held any longer with this earthen fetter of the flesh?" Would God but give us some idea or imperfect glimpse of heaven's glory, how should we be ready to fall into a trance with

Peter! And being a little recovered out of it, what earnest suitors would we be to be caught up forever into the heavenly paradise!

You who are the heirs of glory, be exhorted to work with all your might for God. Love and serve God more intently than others, for He has laid up such things for you as eye has not seen, nor can it enter into man's heart to conceive. 1 Corinthians 15:58: "Always abounding in the work of the Lord, knowing your labor is not in vain in the Lord." Paul had a spirit of activity for God. 1 Corinthians 15:10: "I labored more abundantly than they all." Paul's obedience did not move slowly, like the sun upon the dial, but swiftly, like the sun in the firmament. His eye was upon the crown: "Henceforth is laid up for me a crown of righteousness."

The recompense of reward may add wings to duty and oil to the flame of zeal. What are we that God should encircle us with happiness and not others, that He should (as Jacob) cross His hands, lay His right hand upon us and His left hand upon others? Oh, discriminating grace forever to be adored! How can we ever serve God enough! If there could be tears shed in heaven it would be for this, that we have been so lame in our duty and have brought no more revenues into the heavenly exchequer.

Let this revive and bear up your hearts under all your present sufferings. Acts 20:23: "Bonds and afflictions abide in me." Affliction is the saints' diet drink. Instead of roses, they are crowned with thorns. You may as well separate weight from lead as sufferings from a saint's life. 2 Corinthians 4:8: "We are troubled on every side." Believers are as a ship that has the waves beating on both sides, but this text may buoy them up from sinking. There is glory which outlasts and exceeds all their sufferings.

The saints now drink in a wormwood cup, but shortly they shall drink in a spiced cup and taste the same heavenly nectar as the angels. One day of wearing the celestial crown will abundantly pay for all their sufferings. Romans 8:18: "I recognize that the sufferings of this present time are not worthy to be compared with the glory which shall be revealed in us." The weight of glory makes affliction light. Oh, you saints who are the true birds of paradise, sing in winter. There is glory ahead, and every suffering will be like a grain put in the scale to make your glory weigh heavier. Suffering saints shall have more jewels hung upon their crown.

Let this be an antidote against the fear of death. The day of death is (as Seneca calls it) the birthday of eternity. Believers are not fully happy until death. Death, therefore, is made a part of the inventory (1 Corinthians 3:22). Death is yours. When the mantle of the flesh drops off, the soul ascends in a triumphant chariot. God has promised His people a portion, but it is not paid them until the day of death. It is their Father's good pleasure to give them a kingdom (Luke 12:32), but they cannot see it until death has closed their eyes.

Why then should the saints be troubled at death? Indeed, I wonder not that the wicked are appalled and frightened at the approach of the King of terror. They are in debt to God's justice, and death, as God's sergeant, arrests them and drags them before the divine tribunal. But why should any of God's

children be under such consternation and have
trembling of heart? What hurt does death do to
them? It pulls off their fetters and puts jewels upon
them. It leads them to gates of pearl and rivers of
pleasures. Faith gives a title to heaven, death a possession.

"Go forth, my soul," said Hilarion on his deathbed, "what fearest thou?" Why should the godly
dread their privilege? Is a prince afraid to cross the
narrow seas who is sure to be crowned as soon as he
comes to shore? This puts roses into the pale face of
death and makes it look more ruddy and amiable. It
crowns the saints with all the delights of the
empyrean heaven.

I am done with the text and it remains that I
should speak something to the occasion.

It has pleased the all-wise God to take to Himself
lately that reverend and faithful minister, Mr. Harry
Stubs, whose death we now commemorate. The
memory of the just is blessed. Fulgentius calls a
good name the godly man's heir; it lives when he is
dead. This man of God has left a sweet savor and
perfume behind in God's church besides his
achievement of human learning. He was enriched
with the knowledge of Christ crucified. Graces exceeds the muses.

He was very humble. Humility is the best garment a minister can preach in. He was one of a
thousand for integrity. The plainer the diamond is,
the richer it is.

He was a grave preacher, and chose rather to
speak solidly than floridly. He spoke as was becom-

ing the oracles of God. Levity is below the majesty of preaching.

He was a painful laborer in God's vineyard. He preached in season and out of season. The souls of people were dearer to him than his life. Praying and preaching were rather his delight than task. He was a burning lamp consuming himself to give light to others.

He preached feelingly. He felt those truths in his own soul which he recommended to his auditors. An unconverted minister is like a lute, making sweet music to others but itself is not sensible. This vessel retained a scent and relish of those sacred truths which he poured out to others.

He lived much by faith and had sweet conversation with God. All the saints have God's heart, but some have more of His company.

He was exemplary in his deportment. Ministers, by virtue of their calling, approach nearer to God (Exodus 19:22). The higher the elements are, the purer they are. The fire is purer than the air. The higher we are by office, the holier we should be. This blessed person deceased lived as an incarnate angel. I may say of him what Basil said of Gregory Nazianzen: he thundered in his doctrine and lightninged in his conversation.

He was charitably minded. I have been credibly informed that out of what little he had gathered together while he was living, he appointed two hundred pounds, which he entrusted to the hands of trustees to be improved annually for the good of the poor to buy them Bibles.

He was of a sweet temper, never fierce, but

against sin. He was devout toward God, affable to his
friends and loving to his relations.

The Lord honored his ministry very much; he
had a double crown. The souls he converted were
his crown of rejoicing, and now he wears a crown of
righteousness. How great a loss have Gloucester-
shire and London of this eminent minister! It has
been told me that he set apart some time every day to
pray for the church of God. He (like Moses) lay in
the breach to turn away wrath. We shall soon grow
poor if we lose such praying friends. During the
time of this good man's sickness, he was asthmatic
and labored much for breath so that he could not
express himself so freely; but what was heard to drop
from him was very savory. He said he had fled to the
city of refuge and recited that Scripture, 2 Timothy
1:12: "I know whom I have believed and I am per-
suaded He is able to keep that which I have committed to Him against that day."

I pray that God will give all who are concerned in
this loss wisdom to improve this present stroke and
make a living sermon of their dead master. He now
enjoys the sight of that God whom he so pathetically
longed for upon his deathbed. He is now into the
upper region above all storms. His body is returned
to dust and his soul to rest. He is enclosed in happiness as the word for "crowning" imparts. He is as
rich as the angels; though he has lost his life, yet
not his crown.

A Plea
for
Alms

(Delivered in a sermon at the Spital before a
solemn assembly of the city on Tuesday
in Easter Week, April 13, 1658)

"But who so hath this world's good and seeth his
brother have need, and shutteth up his bowels of
compassion from him, how dwelleth the love of God
in him?" 1 John 3:17

Dedication

To the Right Honorable Sir Richard Chiverton,
Lord Major; the right worshipful, the sheriffs, with
the rest of the aldermen of the famous city of
London.

My own lack of dexterity and my unfitness to
release this publicly needs some apology. But your
acceptance is my encouragement and the order
from your honorable court carries so much
authority with it as to add some weight to that which
dares not plead worth. I was more inclined to
publish this discourse because, though the theme is
common, yet the practice of it is rare and unusual.
When contentions are never more hot and charity
never more cold, it is a sign that iniquity abounds.
The zeal of our forefathers condemns us; we with
Rachel have better eyes but they with Leah were
more fruitful. We are so far (at least the generality of
men) from building churches and almshouses that
we are more ready to pull them down.

How truth is, in these days, forsaken and charity
forgotten! We may say of many that they are miser-
ably rich; their affections toward public advance-
ments and disbursements are like the scales of the
Leviathan, shut up together as with a closed seal
(Job 41:15). St. Ambrose said that when we relieve
not one whom we see ready to perish with hunger,
we are the cause of his death. If this rule holds true,

there are more guilty of the breach of the sixth
commandment than we are aware of.

When shall we see a resurrection of charity
which seems to lie dead and buried? Surely it will
not be unless God works a miracle upon men's
hearts. May the good Lord by His Spirit cleave the
rocks in our bosoms so that the water of repentance
and the wine of charity may flow forth! Oh, that
England might have that encomium, as once
Athens had, to be the nursery of humanity.

Believe it, charity is the best policy. By helping
others we heal ourselves. Job 29:13: "The blessing of
him that was ready to perish came upon me." As the
poor had Job's alms, so he had their prayers and he
fared better. Christ's poor are favorites of the court
of heaven, and when you give them of your gold they
can unlock heaven by the golden key of prayer and
set God at work on your behalf. The merciful man
has many intercessors, which made Jerome to say
that it is almost impossible that God should not
hear the prayers of so many. Why should there be
the least regret or hesitance in our hearts, and why
should charity stick in the birth? It would be our
glory if it might be said of us as St. Paul speaks of
those evangelical Christians in 1 Thessalonians 4:9:
"As touching brotherly love, ye need not that I write
unto you." Oh, how forgetful are we of that breast of
mercy which feeds us, those golden wings which
cover us! Surely we need to keep a register of God's
favors to us. If we did, we would, as Clement of
Alexandria said, give alms to testify of our gratitude.
But I shall avoid prolixness. This sermon which you
hear with seriousness and affection craves now your

candor and comes under your patronage. What was once said to Aegidius of Norinberg concerning David's words in Psalm 118, the same I say concerning these few notions: they are not so much to be read over as to be lived over. Your liberality to those who are in want will give the best gloss upon the text. The Lord has set you in public places, and that you may become public blessing in your generation, walking in the fear of God and shining forth in a Bible conversation, shall be the prayer of him who is your Honor's worshipful servant in the work of the Lord,

Thomas Watson

A Plea for Alms

"He has dispersed, he has given to the poor,
his righteousness endureth forever."
Psalm 112:9

The prophet David, inspired from heaven in this Psalm, deciphers a good man and describes him in two ways:

1. By his sanctity, and that, first, in general, he is one who fears God (verses 1 and 2). In particular, he is charitably minded (verses 5 and 9).

2. The psalmist describes a godly man by his safety. "He shall not be moved forever" (verse 6). He stands impregnable, being planted on the rock of ages. Though evil times come, he is not terrified. "He shall not be afraid of evil tidings; his heart is fixed, trusting in the Lord" (verse 7). Guilt is the breeder of fear. Isaiah 33:14: "The sinners in Zion are afraid, trembling has surprised the hypocrites and a little thing will frighten." Leviticus 26:36: "The sound of a shaken leaf shall chase them."

It is not affliction without, but sin within that creates fear. It is the wind within the bowels of the earth that makes an earthquake. Religion is the best antidote against these heart-killing fears. The fear of God drives out all other fear. The godly man insults danger. With the Leviathan, he laughs at the shaking of a spear, as in Job 41:29. When there is a

119

tempest abroad, he has music at home. He is settled
by faith as a ship at anchor or as a weight in the center. His heart is fixed, trusting in the Lord.

I shall at this time consider the godly man as he
is described by his sanctity, specified under the notion of charity and munificence in these words: "He
hath dispersed, he hath given to the poor, his righteousness endureth forever."

Mercy is a weighty matter of the law (Matthew
23:23). Never can it more seasonably be pressed than
upon a day of such solemnity wherein we commemorate the noble bounty of many worthy and famous
men, whose acts of beneficence and liberality are
left behind as so many monuments of their piety
and renown to succeeding ages.

Give me leave to open the terms. "He hath dispersed." This is a metaphor taken from husband-
men who scatter and disperse their seed in the furrows of the field, expecting a crop afterwards. So the
good man scatters the precious seed of his charity
abroad, and this seed is not lost but afterwards
springs up into a crop.

"He hath given to the poor." The Hebrew word
for "poor" in Scripture signifies one who is empty or
drawn dry, a metaphor taken from ponds or rivers
that are drawn dry. So the poor are exhausted of
their strength, beauty, and substance. Like ponds,
they are dried up; therefore, they must be filled
again with the silver streams of charity.

"His righteousness." By "righteousness" (as most
agreeable to the context) I understand the work of
inherent grace in the heart, displaying and evidenc-
ing itself in works of mercy and bountifulness.

"Endureth forever." Either, first, the comfort of his righteousness endures; he has sweet peace and satisfaction in his own mind. Or, second, the honor of it endures. According to the Hebrew phrase, the memorial of his goodness stands as a monument of fame not to be forgotten. Third, the reward of his righteousness endures. He reaps the fruit of his charity forever, as Kimchi and others interpret it. The words thus opened fall into these four parts: the benefactor; his bounty—"he hath dispersed"; the object—the poor; and the trophy or insignia of his honor displayed—"His righteousness endureth forever."

Or, if you will, the test consists of two things: the godly man's benignity—"He hath dispersed"; and his benediction—"His righteousness endureth forever."

The observation from the words is this, that a godly man is a liberal man. The Hebrew word for "godly" signifies merciful. The more godly, the more merciful. A good man does not, like the snake, twist within himself; his motion is direct, not circular. He is a publicly diffused blessing in the place where he lives, as in Psalm 37:26. "He is ever merciful and lends." As a nobleman's servant is known by the livery he wears, so is a servant of Christ known by this livery of mercifulness and charity.

There are two channels in which the stream of charity must run: charity to the souls of others and charity to the wants of others.

Charity to the souls of others is a spiritual alm. Indeed, this is the highest kind of charity. The soul is the most precious thing. It is a vessel of honor, a bud of eternity, a spark lighted by the breath of God, a rich diamond set in a ring of clay. The soul has the image of God to beautify it and the blood of God to redeem it. It being, therefore, of so high a descent, sprung from the ancient of days, and of so noble an extraction that charity which is shown to the soul must be the greatest.

This is charity to souls when we see others in their blood and we pity them. If I weep (says Augustine) for that body from which the soul is departed, how should I weep for that soul from which God is departed? This is charity to souls when we see men in the gall of bitterness and we labor by counsel, admonition or reproof to pull them out of their natural estate as the angel did Lot out of Sodom in Genesis 19:16. God made a law (Exodus 23:5) that whosoever saw his enemy's ass lying under a burden should help it. On these words Chrysostom said, "We will help a beast that is fallen under a burden, and shall we not extend relief to those who are fallen under a worse burden of sin?" To let others go on in sin securely is not charity but cruelty. If a man's house were on fire and another should see it and not tell him of it for fear of waking him, would not this be cruelty? Did he not deserve to be enlightened? And when we see the souls of others sleeping the sleep of death and the fire of God's wrath ready to burn about their ears and we are silent, is not this to be accessory to their death?

When there is toleration given that if men wish to go to hell none shall stop them, is this charity to souls?

Oh, I beseech you, if you have any compassion,

strengthen the weak, reduce the wandering, raise up them that are fallen. James 5:20: "He which converteth the sinner from the error of his way shall save a soul from death."

Charity to the wants of others, which this text properly intends, consists of three things: (1) a judicious consideration; (2) a tender commiseration; and (3) a liberal contribution.

A judicious consideration. Psalm 41:1: "Blessed is he that considereth the poor." And you must consider four things:

1. It might have been your own case. You might have stood in need of another's charity and then how welcome and refreshing would those streams have been to you.

2. Consider how sad a condition poverty is. Though Chrysostom calls poverty the highway to heaven, he that keeps this road will go weeping thither. Consider the poor. Behold their tears, their sighs, their dying groans. Look upon the deep furrows made in their faces and consider if there be not reason why you should scatter your seed in these furrows. The poor man feeds upon sorrow, he drinks tears (Psalm 80:5). Like Jacob in a windy night he has the clouds for his canopy and a stone for his pillow. Further, consider that oftentimes poverty becomes not only a cross but a snare. It exposes to much evil which made Agur pray, "Give me not poverty" (Proverbs 30:8). Want puts men upon indirect courses. The poor will venture their souls for money, which is like throwing diamonds at pear trees. If the right would wisely consider this, they might be a means of preventing much sin.

3. Consider why the wise God has suffered an inequality in the world. It is for this very reason, that He would have charity exercised. If all were rich, there would be no need for alms nor could the merciful man have been so well known. If he who travelled to Jericho had not been wounded and left half dead, the good Samaritan who poured wine and oil into his wounds would not have been known.

4. Consider how quickly the balance of providence may turn. We ourselves may be brought to poverty and then it will be no small comfort to us that we relieved others while we were in a capacity to do it. Ecclesiastes 11:2: "Give a portion to seven and also to eight, for thou knowest not what evil shall be upon the earth." We cannot promise ourselves always halcyon days. God knows how soon any of us may change our pasture. The cup which now runs over with wine may be filled with the waters of Marah. Ruth 1:21: "I went out full and the Lord has brought me home again empty." How many have we seen who are like Bajazet and Bellizarius, invested with great lordships and possessions, who have, all of a sudden brought their manor down to a morsel.

It is wisdom in this sense to consider the poor. Remember how soon the scene may alter and we may be put in the poor's dress and, if adversity come, it will rejoice us to think that while we had an estate, we laid it out upon Christ's indigent members.

This is the first thing in charity, a judicious consideration. Second is a tender commiseration, as in Isaiah 58:10: "If thou draw out thy soul to the hungry, bounty begins in pity." The Hebrew word for "mercy" signifies bowels. Christ first had compas-

sion on the multitude (Matthew 15:32), then He
wrought a miracle to feed them. Charity which lacks
compassion is brutish. The brute creatures can relieve us in many ways, but cannot pity us. It is a kind
of cruelty (said Quintilian) to feed one in want and
not to sympathize with him. True religion begets
tenderness. As it melts the heart in tears of contri-
tion towards God, so in bowels of compassion toward others. Isaiah 16:11: "My bowels shall sound
like an harp." When your bowels of pity sound, then
your alms make sweet music in the ears of God.

Third, charity consists of a liberal contribution.
Deuteronomy 15:8: "If there be a poor man within
thy gates thou shalt open thy hand wide unto him."
The Hebrew word in the text signifies a largeness of
bounty. It must be like water that overflows the
banks. If God has enriched you with estates and
made His candle (as Job said) to shine upon your
tabernacle, you must not encircle and engross all to
yourselves, but be as the moon which, having received its light from the sun, lets it shine to the
world. The ancients (as Basil and Lorinus observe)
made oil to be the emblem of charity. The golden
oil of your mercy must, like Aaron's oil, run down
upon the poor which are the lower skirts of the
garment.

This liberal disbursement to the necessities of
others, God commands and grace compels. There is
an express statute in Leviticus 25:35: "If thy brother
be waxen poor and fallen in decay with thee, then
thou shalt relieve him." The Hebrew is, "Thou shalt
strengthen him," or "put under him a silver crutch
when he is falling."

It is worth our observation what great care God took of the poor besides what was given privately. God made many laws for the public and visible relief of the poor, as in Exodus 23:11: "The seventh year thou shall let the land rest and lie still that the poor of thy people may eat." God's intention in this law was that the poor should be liberally provided for. They might freely eat of anything which grew of itself the seventh year, whether of herbs, vines, or olive trees.

Someone may ask how the poor could live only on these fruits, there being (as it is probable) no corn growing then. Cajetan is of the opinion they lived by selling these fruits and converting them into money; so they lived upon the price of the fruits.

There is another law made in Leviticus 19:9: "And when ye reap the harvest of your land, thou shalt not wholly reap the corners of thy field, neither shalt thou gather the gleanings of thy harvest." See how God indulged the poor. Some corners of the field were, for the poor's sake, to be left uncut; and when the owners reaped they must not go too near the earth with their sickle. Something like an after-crop must be left. The shorter ears of corn, and such as lay bending to the ground, were to be reserved for the poor.

God made another law in favor of the poor, Deuteronomy 14:28–29: "At the end of three years thou shalt bring forth the tithe of the increase the same year and thou shalt lay it up in thy gates, and the Levites and the fatherless and the widow which are within thy gates shall come and eat and be satis-

fied." The Hebrews write that every third year, besides the first tithe given to Levi, which was called
the perpetual tithe (Numbers 18:21), the Jews set
apart another tithe of their increase for the use of
the widows and orphans; and that was called the
tithe of the poor. Besides at the Jew's solemn festi-
vals, the poor were to have a share (Deuteronomy
16:11).

Relieving the necessities was commanded under
the law, and it stands in force under the gospel. 1
Timothy 6:17–18: "Charge them that be rich in this
world that they do good, that they be rich in good
works." It is not only a counsel but a charge, and
non-attendance to it runs men into a gospel offense.

Thus we have seen the mind of God in this particular charity. Let all good Christians comment
upon it in their practice. What benefit is there of
gold while it is emboweled and locked up in the
mine? How is it better to have a great estate if it is so
hoarded and cloistered up as to never see the light?

As God commands us, so grace compels us to
works of mercy and beneficence. 2 Corinthians 5:14:
"The love of Christ constrains us." Grace comes with
majesty upon the heart. It is not in sermon, but
virtue. Grace does not lie as a sleepy habit in the
soul, but will put forth itself in vigorous and glorious actions. Grace can no more be concealed than
fire. Like new wine, it will have vent. Grace does not
lie in the heart as a stone in the earth, but as seed in
the earth; and it will spring up into good works.

It may serve to justify the Church of England
against the calumny of malevolent men. Julian up-
braided the Christians that they were Solifidians;

and the church of Rome lays upon us the aspersion that we are against good works. Indeed, we plead not for the *merit* of them, but we are for the *use* of them (Titus 3:14). Let us also learn to maintain good works for necessary use. We preach they are needful because of both precept and mediator.

We read the angels had wings and hands under their wings (Ezekiel 1:8). It may be a hieroglyphic emblem of this truth: Christians must not only have the wings of faith to fly, but hands under their wings to work the works of mercy. This is a faithful saying, and these things I will that you maintain constantly that they who have believed in God might "be careful to maintain good works" (Titus 3:8).

The lamp of faith must be filled with the oil of charity. Faith alone justifies but justifying faith is not alone. You may as well separate weight from lead or heat from fire as works from faith. Good works, though they are not the causes of salvation, yet they are evidences. Though they are not the foundation, yet they are the superstructure. Faith must not be built upon works, but works must be built upon faith. Romans 7:4: "Ye are married to another that you should bring forth fruit unto God." Faith is the spouse which marries Christ and good works are the children which faith bears. For the vindication of the doctrine of our church and in the honor of good works, I shall lay down these four aphorisms.

1. Works are distinct from faith. It is vain to imagine that works are included in faith as the diamond is enclosed in the ring. They are distinct, as the sap in the vine is different from the clusters that grow upon it.

2. Works are the touchstone of faith. "Show me thy faith by thy works" (James 2:18). Works are faith's letters of credence to show. If (said Bernard) you see a man full of good works, then, by the rule of charity, you are not to doubt his faith. We judge the health of the body by the pulse, where the blood stirs and operates. Christian, judge the health of your faith by the pulse of charity. It is with faith as with a deed in law. To make a deed in law valid, there are three things required: the writing, the seal, and the witnesses. So for the trial and confirmation of faith, there must be these three things: the writing (the Word of God), the seal (the Spirit of God), and the witnesses (good works). Bring your faith to this Scripture touchstone. Faith justifies works; works testify to faith.

3. Works honor faith as the fruit adorns the tree. Let the liberality of your hand (said Clement of Alexandria) be the ornament of your faith, and wear it as a holy bracelet about your wrists. Job 29:14–15: "I was eyes to the blind and feet to the lame, I put on righteousness and it clothed me; my judgment was as a robe and a diadem." While Job was pleading the cause of the poor, this was the ensign of his honor; it clothed him as a robe and crowned him as a diadem. This is what takes off the odium and obloquy from religion, and makes others speak well of holiness when they see good works as handmaids waiting upon this queen.

4. Good works are in some sense more excellent than faith in two respects:

First, because they are of a more noble diffusive nature. Though faith is more needful for us, yet works are more beneficial to others. Faith is a receptive grace, all for self-interest, and it moves within its own sphere. Works are for the good of others. It is a more blessed thing to give than to receive.

Second, good works are more visible and conspicuous than faith. Faith is a more hidden grace. It may lie hidden in the heart and may not be seen, but when works are joined with it, it shines forth in its native beauty. Though a garden is decked with flowers, they are not seen until the light comes. So the heart of a Christian may be enriched with faith, but it is like a flower in the night. It is not seen until works come. When this light shines before men, then faith appears in its orient colors.

REPROOF. If this is the effigy of a good man, that he is of a charitable disposition, then it sharply reproves those who are far from this temper, who are all for gathering but not for dispersing. They move only within the circle of their own interests, but do not indulge the necessities of others. They have a flourishing estate, but, like the man in the gospel, they have a withered hand and cannot stretch it out to good uses. These are like the churl Nabal in 1 Samuel 25:11: "Shall I take my bread and my water and give it unto men whom I know not whence they be?" It was said of the Emperor Pertinaz that he had a large empire, but a narrow, scanty heart.

There was a temple at Athens which was called the temple of mercy. It was dedicated to charitable uses, and the greatest reproach to upbraid one that he had never been in the temple of mercy. It is the greatest disgrace to a Christian to be unmerciful.

Covetous men, while they enrich themselves, debase themselves, setting up a monopoly and committing idolatry with mammon, thus making themselves lower than men as God made them lower than His angels.

In the time of pestilence it is sad to have your houses shut up, but it is worse to have your hearts shut up. Covetous persons are like the Leviathan in Job 41:24: their hearts are firm as a stone. You may as well extract oil out of a flint as the golden oil of charity out of their flinty hearts. The philosopher said that the coldness of the heart is a presage of death. When men's affections toward works of mercy are frozen, this coldness of heart is ominous and sadly portends that they are dead in sin. We read in the law that the shellfish was accounted as unclean. This is probably because the meat of it was enclosed in the shell and was hard to come by. They are to be reckoned among the unclean who enclose all their estate within the shell of their own cabinet and will not let others be the better for it. How many have lost their souls by being so saving!

There are some who, perhaps, will give the poor good words and that is all. James 2:15–16: "If a brother or sister be naked and destitute of food and one of you say to them, 'Depart in peace, be ye warmed and filled,' notwithstanding you give them not those things which are needful, what doth it profit?" Good words are but a cold kind of charity. The poor cannot live as the chameleon upon this air. Let your words be as smooth as oil, yet they will not heal the wounded. Let them drop as the honeycomb, they will not feed the hungry. "Though I

speak with the tongue of angels and have not charity, I am but as a tinkling cymbal" (1 Corinthians
13:1).

It is better to be charitable as a saint than elo-
quent as an angel. Such as are cruel to the poor, let
me tell you, you "unChristian" yourselves. Unmercifulness is the sin of the heathen, Romans 1:31.
While you put off the bowels of charity, you put off
the badge of Christianity. James speaks a sad word in
James 2:13: "for he shall have judgment without
mercy that showed no mercy." Dives denied Lazarus
a crumb of bread and Dives was denied a drop of water at the last day. Behold the sinner's indictment in
Matthew 25:42: "I was hungry and ye gave Me no
meat, I was thirsty and ye gave Me no drink." Christ
does not say, "You took away My meat," but "You *gave*
Me none. You did not feed My members." Then follows the sentence, "Depart from Me, ye cursed."

If Christ's poor come to your doors and you bid
them depart from you, the time may come when you
shall knock at heaven's gate and Christ will say, "Go
from My door; depart from Me, ye cursed."

In short, covetousness is a foolish sin. God gave
the rich man in the gospel the appellation, "Thou
fool" (Luke 12:20). The covetous man does not enjoy
what he possesses. He embitters his own life. He oc-
cupies himself with care either how to get, or how to
increase, or how to secure an estate; and what is the
issue and result? Often, as a just reward of sordid
penuriousness, God blasts and withers him in his
outward estate. The saying of Gregory Nazianzen is
to be seriously weighed: "God many times lets the
thief take away and the moth consume that which is

injuriously and uncharitably withheld from the poor."

Before I leave this, I am sorry that any who pass for honest men should be brought into the indictment, I mean, that any professors should be impeached as guilty of this sin of covetousness and unmercifulness. Sure I am that God's elect put on bowels (Colossians 3:12). I tell you, these devout misers are the reproach of Christianity. They are warts and spots on the face of religion. Truly, I know not well what to make of them!

Aelian, in his history, reports that in India there is a griffin having four feet and wings, his bill like the eagle's. It is hard to decide whether to rank him among the beasts or the fowl. So I may say of penurious votaries: they have the wings of profession, by which they seem to fly to heaven, but the feet of beasts walking on the earth and even licking the dust. It is hard to know where to rank these, whether among the godly or the wicked. Take heed that, if your religion will not destroy your covetousness, at last your covetousness does not destroy your religion.

The Fabler tells us a story of the hedgehog that came to the conies' burrows in stormy weather and desired harbor, promising that he would be a quiet guest. Once he had gotten entertainment, he set up his prickles and never left until he had thrust the poor conies out of their burrows. So it is with covetousness: though it has many fair pleas to insinuate and wind itself into the heart, as soon as you let it in this thorn will never stop pricking until it has choked all good beginnings and thrust all religion out of your heart.

EXHORTATION 1. I beseech all who hear me
this day to put on bowels of mercies, to be ready to
indulge the miseries and necessities of others.
Ambrose calls charity the sum of Christianity, and
the Apostle James (1:27) makes it the very definition
of religion: "Pure religion and undefiled before God
and the Father is this, to visit the fatherless and the
widows in their affliction." The poor are, as it were,
in the grave; the comfort of their life is buried. Help
with your merciful hands to raise them out of the
sepulchre. God sends His springs into the valleys
(Psalm 104:10). Let the springs of your charity run
among the valleys of poverty. Your sweetest and most
benign influences should fall upon the lower
grounds. What is all your seeming devotion without
bounty and mercifulness?

I have known many (said Basil) who pray and
fast, but relieve not such as are in distress. They are
for a zeal that puts them to no charges. What are
they the better (said he) for all their seeming virtue?

We read the incense was to be laid upon the fire
(Leviticus 16:13). The flame of devotion must be perfumed with the incense of charity. Aaron was to have
a bell and a pomegranate. The pomegranate (as
some of the learned observe) was a symbol of good
works. They lack the pomegranate (said Gregory
Nazianzen) who have no good works. The wise men
not only bowed the knee to Christ, but presented
Him with gold, myrrh, and frankincense (Matthew
2:11). Pretenses of zeal are insufficient. We must not
only worship Christ, but bestow something upon

His members. This is to present Christ with gold
and frankincense. Isaac would not bless Jacob by the
voice, but he felt and handled him, and supposing
them to be Esau's hands he blessed him. God will
not bless you by your voice, your loud prayers, or
your devout discourses, but if He feels Esau's hands,
if your hands have wrought good works, then He
will bless you.

Let me exhort you, therefore, to deeds of mercy.
Let your fingers drop with the myrrh of liberality.
Sow your golden seed. In this sense, it is lawful to
put out your money when you lay it out for good
uses. Remember that excellent saying of Augustine,
"Give those things to the poor which you cannot
keep that you may receive those things which you
cannot lose."

There are many occasions for exercising your pious charity: hear the orphan's cry; pity the widow's
tears. There are some who want employment, so it
would do well to set their wheel a-going. Others who
are past employment are as eyes to the blind and feet
to the lame. Some whole families will sink if your
merciful hands do not help to shore them up.

I cannot be unmindful of the universities which
are the nurseries of the church. They may be compared to that Persian tree Theophrastus speaks of,
which buds, blossoms and bears ripe fruit at the
same time. Oh, let these plants be watered with your
silver drops! Cast not salt, but gold into these
springs that from thence may flow forth many celestial streams both of learning and piety to refresh
this city of our God.

Before I come to press you with arguments to lib-

erality and munificence, there are three objections
in the way which I shall endeavor to remove.

OBJECTION 1. "We may give, and so in time ourselves come to want."

Let Basil answer this: "Wells which have their water drawn spring ever more freely." Proverbs 11:25:
"The liberal soul shall be made fat." Luther speaks
of a monastery in Austria which was very rich while
it gave annually to the poor, but when it left off giving the monastery began to decay. There is nothing
lost by doing our duty. An estate may be imparted yet
not impaired. The flowers yield honey to the bee, yet
their own fruit is not harmed. When the candle of
prosperity shines upon us, we may give light to our
neighbor who is in the dark and have never the less
light ourselves. Whatever is disbursed to pious uses,
God brings it in some other way, as the loaves mul-
tiplied in breaking, or as the widow's oil increased
by pouring it out in 1 Kings 17:16.

OBJECTION 2. "I cannot do so much as others—
erect churches, build hospitals, augment libraries,
or maintain scholars at the university."

If you cannot do much, do something. The widow's two mites cast into the treasury were accepted
in Luke 21. God (as Chrystostom observed) looked
not at the smallness of her gift, but the largeness of
her heart. In the law, for him who could not bring a
lamb for an offering, it sufficed if he brought two
turtledoves. We read in Exodus 35 that the people
brought gold and silver and goat's hair to the building of the tabernacle. On which place, said Origen,
"I desire, Lord, to bring something to the building
of Thy temple; if not gold to make the mercy seat, if

not silk to make the curtains, yet a little goat's hair that I may not be found in the number of those that have brought nothing to Thy temple."

OBJECTION 3. "I have nothing to bestow upon the necessities of others."

Do you have money to feed your pride and nothing to relieve the poor members of Christ? Let us admit this excuse to be real, that you have no such estate, yet you may do something wherein you may express your mercy to the poor. You may sympathize with them, pray for them, or speak a word of comfort to them. Isaiah 40:2 says, "Speak ye comfortably to Jerusalem." If you can give them no gold, you may speak a word in season which may be as apples of gold in pictures of silver. You may be helpful to the poor by stirring up others who do have estates to relieve them. If a man is hungry, the wind will not fill him, but it can blow the sails of the mill and make it grind corn for the use of man. So, though you have no estate yourself to help those in want, you may stir up others to help them. You may blow the sails of their affections, causing them to show mercy, and so may help your brother by a proxy.

EXHORTATION 2. Having answered these objections, let me pursue the exhortation to mercy and liberality. I shall lay down several arguments which I desire you to weigh in the balance of reason and conscience.

To be diffusively good is the great end of our creation. Ephesians 2:10 says we are created in Christ Jesus unto good works. Every creature answers the end of its creation. The star shines, the bird sings, the plant bears, the end of life is service. He who does not answer his end in respect of usefulness cannot enjoy his end in respect of happiness. Many, says Seneca, have been long in the world, but have not lived. They have done no good. A useless person serves for nothing but to cumber the ground and, because he is barren of figs, he shall be fruitful in curses.

By this we resemble God who is a God of mercy. He is said to delight in mercy (Micah 7:18). "His mercies are over all His works" (Psalm 145:9). He requites good for evil. Like the clouds which receive ill vapors from us, but return them to us again in sweet showers, there is not a creature alive but tastes of the mercies of God. "Every bird," said Ambrose, "does in its kind sing hymns of praise to God for His bounty, but men and angels, in a more peculiar manner, taste the cream and quintessence of God's mercies."

What temporal mercies have you received? Every time you draw your breath you suck in mercy; every bit of bread you eat, the hand of mercy carves it to you. You never drink but in a golden cup of mercy. What spiritual mercies has God invested some of you with? Pardon, adoption, saving mercy. The picture of God's mercy can never be drawn to the full. You cannot take the breadth of His mercy, for it is infinite; nor the height of it, for it reaches above the clouds; nor the length of it, for it is from everlasting to everlasting (Psalm 103:17). The works of mercy are the glory of the Godhead. Moses prayed, "Lord, show me Thy glory." God said, "I will make all My goodness to pass before thee" (Exodus 33:18–19).

God accounts Himself most glorious in the shining
robes of His mercy. Now, by works of mercy, we resemble the God of mercy. We are bid to draw our
lines according to Luke 6:36: "Be merciful as your
Father also is merciful."

Alms are a sacrifice. Hebrews 13:16: "To do good
and to communicate, forget not, for with such sacrifices God is well pleased." When you are distributing
to the poor, it is as if you were praying, as if you were
worshipping God. There are two sorts of sacrifices:
expiatory (the sacrifice of Christ's blood) and gratu-
latory (the sacrifice of alms). This, said holy
[Richard] Greenham, is more acceptable to God
than any other sacrifice. Acts 10:4: "The angel said
to Cornelius, 'Thy alms are come up for a memorial
before God.' " The backs of the poor are the altar on
which this sacrifice is to be offered up.

We ourselves live upon alms. Other creatures liberally contribute to our necessities. The sun has not
its light for itself, but for us. It enriches us with its
golden beams; the earth brings us a fruitful crop to
show how joyful a mother is in bringing forth. The
Psalmist says, "The valleys are covered with corn;
they shout for joy, they also sing" (Psalm 65:13). One
creature gives us wool, another oil, another silk. We
are fain to go begging to the creation. Shall every
creature be for the good of man, and man only be
for himself?

We are to extend our liberality by virtue of a
shared membership. Isaiah 58:7: "That thou hide
not thyself from thy own flesh." The poor are fellow
members of the same body. The members, by a law
of equity and sympathy, contribute one to another.

The eye conveys light to the body, the heart blood, the head spirits. It is a dead member in the body which does not communicate to the rest. Thus it is also in the body politic. Let no man think it is too far below him to mind the wants and necessities of others. It is a pity that the hand should be cut off which disdains to pluck a thorn out of the foot. It is spoken in the honor of that renowned princess, the Empress of Theodosius the Great, that she herself visited the sick and prepared relief for them with her own imperial hands.

We are not lords of an estate, but stewards. Soon we may hear, "Give an account of thy stewardship, for thou mayest be no longer steward" (Luke 16:2). An estate is a talent to trade with. It is as dangerous to hide our talent as to spend it (Matthew 25:25–30). If the covetous man keeps his gold too long it will begin to rust, and the rust of it will witness against him.

Recall the examples of others who have been famous and renowned for acts of charity. Our Lord Christ was a great example of charity. He was not more full of merit than bounty. Trajan, the emperor, rent off a piece of his own robe to wrap his soldiers' wounds. Christ did more: He made a medicine of His body and blood to heal us. Isaiah 53:5: "By His stripes we are healed." Here was a pattern of charity without parallel.

The Jews are noted in this respect. It is a rabbinical observation that those who live devoutly among the Jews distribute a tenth part of their estate among the poor, and they give freely (said Philo, the Jew) as if by giving they hope to receive some great gratuity.

Now if the Jews are so devoted to works of mercy, who live without priest, without temple, without Messiah, shall not we much more who profess our faith in the blessed Messiah?

Let me tell you of some heathens. I have read that Titus Vespasian, who was so inured to works of mercy that, remembering he had given nothing that day, cried out, "I have lost a day." It is reported of some of the Turks that they have servants whom they employ on purpose to inquire what poor they have, and then send relief to them. The Turks have a saying in their Koran that if men knew what a blessed thing it was to distribute alms rather than spare, they would give some of their own flesh to relieve the poor; and shall not a Christian's creed be better than a Turk's Koran?

But, right honorable and beloved, we are not left this day without witness. I desire to speak it to the glory of God and the renown of this city that there has been, both in the days of our worthy progenitors and still to this day among many of you, a spirit of sympathy and compassion.

When poor indigent creatures have been as Moses, laid in the ark of bulrushes, ready to sink in the waters of affliction, you have sent temporal favors to them, and have drawn them out of the waters with a golden cord. When they have been ready to make their own grave, you have built them hospitals. The milk of your charity has nursed them, and while they have sat under your vines they have eaten the sweet grape. We read that they showed Peter the garments and coats which Dorcas made (Acts 9:39). May we not this day behold the coats which have been made to clothe the indigent? Go on still to do worthily in Ephrata, and, by your acts of munificence, to emblazen your coat of arms and eternalize your fame.

I shall use one more argument to persuade to charity, and that is the reward which follows alms deeds. Giving alms is a glorious work, and, let me tell you, it is no unfruitful work. They who sow mercy shall reap mercy. Whatsoever is disbursed to the poor is given to Christ. Matthew 25:40: "Inasmuch as ye have done it to one of the least of these, My brethren, ye have done it unto Me." The poor man's hand is Christ's treasury, and there is nothing lost which is put there.

There is a reward in this life. The charitable man is crowned with a blessing. He is:

Blessed in his person. Psalm 41:1: "Blessed is he that considers the poor." God casts a favorable aspect upon him.

Blessed in his name. So it is in the text: his horn shall be exalted with honor. Also Psalm 112:6: "He shall be had in everlasting remembrance." His name shall be gloriously embalmed.

Blessed in his estate. Proverbs 11:25: "The liberal soul shall be made fat." He shall not only have the venison, but the blessing.

Blessed in his posterity. Psalm 37:26: "He is ever merciful and lendeth, and his seed is blessed." He shall not only leave an estate behind, but a blessing behind to his children; and God will see that the estate shall not be cut off.

Blessed in his negotiations. Deuteronomy 15:10: "For this thing the Lord thy God shall bless thee in all

thy works and in all that thou puttest thine hand
unto." The charitable man shall be blessed in his
building, planting, journeying; whatever he is about
a blessing shall empty itself upon him. He shall be a
prosperous man; the honeycomb of a blessing shall
be still dropping upon him.

Blessed with long life. Psalm 41:2: "The Lord will preserve him and keep him alive." He has helped to
keep others alive and God will keep him alive. Is
there anything then lost by charity? It spins out the
silver thread of life. Many are taken away the sooner
for their unmercifulness; because their hearts are
not strengthened, their lives are shortened.

The great reward is in the life to come. Aristotle
joined these two together, liberality and utility. God
will reward the merciful man, though not *for* his
works, yet according *to* his works. Revelation 20:12: "I
saw the dead, small and great, stand before God, and
the books were opened and the dead were judged
out of those things which were written in the books
according to their works." As God has a bottle to put
your tears in, so He has a book to write your alms in.
As God will put a veil over His people's sins, so He
will set a crown upon their works. The way to lay up
is to lay out. Other parts of your estate you leave behind, but that which is given to Christ's poor is
hoarded up in heaven! That is a blessed kind of giving which, though it makes the purse lighter, makes
the crown heavier.

Whatever alms you distribute, you shall have
good security. Proverbs 19:17: "He that gives to the
poor lends to the Lord, and that which he hath
given will He pay him again." There is God's coun-

termand to save you unhurt, which is better security
than any public faith. Yet here is our unbelief and
atheism: we will not take God's bond. We commonly
put our deeds of mercy among our desperate debts.
You shall be paid with an abundance. For a
wedge of gold which you have parted with, you shall
have a weight of glory. For a cup of cold water, you
shall have rivers of pleasure which run at God's
right hand forevermore. The interest comes to infinitely more than the principal. Pliny writes of a
country in Africa where the people, for every bushel
of seed they sow, receive a hundred and fifty-fold increase. For every penny you drop into Christ's treasury, you shall receive above a thousandfold increase. Your after-crop of glory will be so great that,
though you are still reaping, you will never be able
to end the whole harvest. Let this persuade rich men
to honor the Lord with their substance.

Before I conclude, let me lay down some rules
briefly concerning your charity that it may be the
sacrifice of a sweet-smelling savor to God.
RULE 1. Your charity must be free. Deuteronomy
15:10: "Thou shalt give, and thy heart shall not be
grieved." That is, you shall not be troubled at parting with your money. He who gives grievingly gives
grudgingly. Charity must flow like spring water. The
heart must be the spring, the hand the pipe, the
poor the cistern. God loves a cheerful giver. Be not
like the crab which has all the juice squeezed and
pressed out. You must not give to the poor as if you
were delivering your purse on the highway. Charity
without alacrity is rather a fine than an offering. It is

rather doing penance than giving alms. Charity must be like the myrrh which drops from the tree without cutting or forcing.

RULE 2. We must give that which is our own. Isaiah 58:7: "To deal thy bread to the hungry." The word for "alms" in the Syriac signifies "justice". To show that alms must be of that which is justly gotten, the Scripture puts them together. "To do justice, to love mercy" (Micah 6:8), we must not make a sacrilege of sacrifice. Isaiah 61:8: "For I, the Lord, love judgment, I hate robbery for burnt offering." He who shall build a hospital with goods ill-gotten displays the insignia of his pride and sets up the monument of his shame.

RULE 3. Do all in Christ and for Christ. Labor that your persons may be in Christ. We are accepted in Him (Ephesians 1:6). Origen, Chrysostom, and Peter Martyr affirm that the best works not springing from a root of faith are lost.

The Pelagians thought to have posed Augustine with the question whether it was sin in the heathen to clothe the naked. Augustine answered rightly, "The doing of good is not in itself simply evil, but, proceeding of infidelity, it becomes evil." Titus 1:15: "To them that are unbelieving is nothing pure." That fruit is most sweet and genuine which is brought forth in the vine (John 15:4). Outside of Christ all our alms deeds are but the fruit of the wild olive. They are not good works, but dead works.

RULE 4. Do all for Christ, for His sake, that you may testify to your love for Him. Love mellows and ripens our alms deeds; it makes them a precious perfume to God. As Mary, out of love, brought her oint-

ments and sweet spices to anoint Christ's dead body,
so, out of love for Christ, bring your ointments and
anoint His living body, His saints and members.

RULE 5. Works of mercy are to be done in humility. Away with ostentation. The worm breeds in
the fairest fruit, the moth in the finest cloth. Pride
will be creeping into our best things. Beware of this
dead fly in the box of ointment. When Moses' face
shone, he put a veil over it; so while your light
shines before men, and they see your good works,
cover yourselves with the veil of humility. As the
silkworm weaves her curious works, and hides herself within the silk and is not seen, so we should
hide ourselves from pride and vainglory.

It was the sin of the Pharisees that, while they
were distributing alms, they blew the trumpet
(Matthew 6:2). They did not give their alms, but sold
them for applause. A proud man casts his bread
upon the waters as the fisherman casts his rod upon
the waters: he angles for vainglory.

I have read of Cosmos Medices, a rich citizen of
Florence, who confessed to a near friend of his that
he built so many magnificent structures, and spent
so much on scholars and libraries, not for any love
of learning, but to raise up for himself the trophies
of fame and renown. A humble soul denies himself,
yea, even annihilates himself. He thinks how little it
is he can do for God, and, if he could do more, it
would be but a due debt. Therefore he looks upon
all his works as if he had done nothing.

The saints are brought in at the last day as dis-
owning their works of charity. Matthew 25:37: "Lord,
when did we see Thee hungry and fed Thee, or

thirsty and gave Thee drink?" A good Christian not only empties his hand of alms, but empties his heart of pride while he raises the poor out of the dust. He lays himself in the dust. Works of mercy must be like the cassia, which is a sweet spice but grows low. Dispose your alms prudently. It is said of the merciful man that he orders his affairs with discretion (Psalm 112:5). There is a great deal of wisdom in distinguishing between those who have sinned themselves into poverty and those who, by the hand of God, are brought into poverty. Discretion in the distribution of alms consists in two things: in finding a fit object and in taking the fit season.

In finding a fit object. Give to those who are in most need. Raise the hedge where it is lowest; feed the lamp which is going out. Give to those who may probably be most serviceable. Though we bestow cost and dressing upon a weak plant, yet not upon a dead plant. Breed up such as may help to build the house of Israel (Ruth 4:11). Those who may be pillars in church and state, not caterpillars, make your charity to blush.

In taking the fit season. Give to charitable uses in time of health and prosperity. Distribute your silver and gold to the poor before the silver cord is loosed or the golden bowl is broken (Ecclesiastes 12:6). Make your hands your executors, not as some who reserve all they give till the term of life is ready to expire. Truly, what is then bestowed is not given away, but taken away by death. It is not charity but necessity. Do not marry yourselves to money so that you are resolved that nothing shall part you but death. Be not like the meddler who is never good until he is rotten. A covetous man may be compared to a Christmas box: he receives money, but parts with none until death breaks this box in pieces, and then the silver and gold come tumbling out. Give in time of health. These are the alms which God takes notice of, and, as Calvin said, He puts into His book of accounts.

RULE 6. Give thankfully. They should be more thankful who give alms than they who receive. We should, said Nazianzen, give a thank offering to God that we are in the number of givers and not receivers. Bless God for a willing mind. To have not only an estate but a heart is a matter of congratulation. Set the crown of your thankfulness upon the head of free grace.

The

One Thing

Necessary

(Preached in a sermon at St. Paul's before
before the Right Honorable Lord Mayor,
and the Aldermen of the City of
London, August 31, 1656)

"How shall we escape if we neglect
so great salvation?" Hebrews 2:3

Dedication

_____

To the Right Honorable John Dethick,
Lord Mayor of the City of London

Right Honorable,

It was not in my thoughts to have published this sermon (I looked upon it as too homespun), but it was your Lordship's request to me at the first, and I have since received an invitation from your honorable court to that purpose. I knew not how to deny, lest while I shunned your loving commands I should fall under your just censure. My Lord, it was my design in this sermon to call you off from the empty, high-flown notions and litigious disputes of these times to look after that which is more solid, and wherein, I am sure, every man is very nearly concerned, namely, the working out of his salvation. It is a work that may call forth the most spiritual, vigorous actings of the soul in the prosecution of it. That work needs to be well done which is for eternity.

My Lord, this is the true wisdom: to be wise unto salvation (2 Timothy 3:15). By this godly policy we shall go beyond all the politicians of the times. We shall escape hell. We shall be raised to the true seat of honor. God will be our Father, Christ our Brother, the Spirit our Comforter, the angels our companions. When we die, we shall carry a good conscience with us and leave a good name behind us. I shall not further expatiate. I desire that this sermon may come under your Honor's patronage. Some little addition you will find in the end which I had prepared for you, but lacked time to serve it in. May the Lord ennoble you with His Spirit, and crown you with soul prosperity, which shall be the prayer of him who is,

Your Honor's in all gospel service,
Thomas Watson

From my study at St. Stephen's,
October 15, 1656

The One Thing Necessary

"Work out your own salvation with fear and trembling." Philippians 2:12

If there is anything excellent, it is salvation. If there is anything necessary, it is working out salvation. If there is any tool to work with, it is holy fear: "work out your salvation with fear."

The words are a grave and serious exhortation, needful not only for those Christians who lived in the time of the Apostles, but it may be fitly calculated for the meridian of this age wherein we live.

In the text observe first the manner of insinuation:

"My beloved." The Apostle labored by all means to ingratiate and wind himself into the hearts of the Philippians. He prescribes a gospel pill and dips it in sugar that it may go down better. He labors to possess the Philippians of this maxim, that whatever he spoke to them about their souls was purely in love. Sometimes he steeps his words in tears and speaks weeping (Philippians 3:18). Sometimes he dips them in honey. Paul knew how to reprove. It was part of his office and a piece of his spiritual surgery. "Rebuke them sharply" (Titus 1:13), or, as the Greek says, "cuttingly." But, when he had finished lancing, he knew how to pour wine and oil into the wound. He holds forth the breast as a nurse, and is willing to impart not only his sermon to the people, but his soul (1 Thessalonians 2:7–8).

And herein the Apostle Paul sets an example for all the ministers of Christ. Their hearts must be fired not with heat of passion but with love towards their people. They are Christ's ambassadors and must come with an olive branch of peace in their mouths. "If I speak with the tongue of angels, and have not love, I am as sounding brass, and a tinkling cymbal" (1 Corinthians 13:1). It is better to love as a pastor than to speak as an angel. Love is that flower of delight which should grow in the heart and send forth its perfume in the lips of every minister. Those who come in a spirit of meekness to their people are likely to do the most good. Knotty hearts will be soonest worked on by love. The fire will go where the wedge cannot. The thunderbolt may break, but the sun melts. When love sends forth its sweet influence, it melts a sinner's heart into tears. The joints being hard and stiff, rubbing them with oil makes them supple. The best way to soften a hard heart and make it tender is to ply it with this oil of love. And so much for the manner of insinuation, "My beloved."

I proceed now to the exhortation itself, "Work out your own salvation with fear and trembling," which words branch into three particulars:

First, the act: "work out." Second, the object: "your own salvation." Third, the mode or manner how we should work it out: "with fear and trembling." I shall speak principally of the first two, and draw in the other briefly in the application.

The proposition is this: it should be a Chris-

tian's great work to be working out his salvation.
The great God has put us into the world as a vineyard, and here is the work He has set us about: the
working out of salvation. There is a parallel Scripture to this in 2 Peter 1:10: "Give diligence to make
your calling and election sure." When estate,
friends, or life cannot be made sure, let this be made
sure. The Greek word signifies "to study" or "to beat
the brains about a thing." The word in the text,
"work out," implies two things. First, it implies a
shaking off of spiritual sloth. Sloth is a pillow on
which many have slept the sleep of death. And, second, it implies a uniting and rallying together of all
the powers of our souls that we may intend the business of salvation. God enacted a law in paradise that
no man should eat of the tree of life but in the sweat
of his brow.

That which is called "working" in the text has
various appellations in Scripture. First, it is sometimes called "striving." Luke 13:24: "Strive to enter in
at the narrow gate." Strive as if in agony or a bloody
sweat.

Second, it is sometimes called "seeking."
Matthew 6:33: "Seek ye first the kingdom of God," as
a man who has lost a treasure seeks diligently for it.
We have lost salvation. Adam, by eating of the tree of
knowledge, lost the tree of life. Now seek; take
David's candle and lantern and seek for salvation.
The word "seek," as a learned writer notes, signifies
"to pursue a thing with inflamed desires," as a con-
demned man desires a pardon.

Third, it is sometimes called "running in a race."
1 Corinthians 9:24: "So run that ye may obtain." The

Apostle seems to allude to the games of Olympus
which were celebrated every fifth year in honor of
Jupiter. In those games they put forth all their
strength. It is a long race from earth to heaven, so
lay aside all the weights of sin which will hinder you
in the race and reach forward with a winged swiftness to lay hold upon the mark.

Fourth, it is sometimes called "offering violence
to heaven." Matthew 11:12: "The kingdom of heaven
suffers violence." There must not only be diligence,
but there must be violence. We must not only pray,
but pray fervently (James 5:16). We must not only repent, but be zealous and repent (Revelation 3:19); we
must not only love, but be sick of love (Song of Solomon 2:5). This is offering violence. The Greek word
is a metaphor taken from a castle that holds out in a
siege and will not be taken unless it is stormed. So
the kingdom of heaven holds out against a supine,
lazy Christian, and will not be taken but by storm.

REASONS. I now proceed to the reasons enforc-
ing this holy sweat and industry about salvation, and
they are three. We must work out our salvation because of the difficulty of this work, the rareness of
this work, and the possibility of this work.

REASON 1. *The difficulty of this work.* It is a work
that may make us labor to the going down of the
sun of our life. Now this difficulty about the work of
salvation will appear in four ways:

First, from the nature of the work. There is a
metamorphosis to be worked. The heart must be
changed; it is the very nursery of sin. It is the maga-
zine where all the weapons of unrighteousness lie. It

is a lesser hell. The heart is full of antipathy against
God. It is angry with converting grace. Now, that the
bypass of the heart should be changed, what a work
is this! How we should beg Christ, that He who
turned water into wine would turn the water, or
rather the poison, of nature into the wine of grace!

Second, the current of life is to be altered. That
the tide of sin, which before ran so strong, should
be turned is not easy. That the sinner, who before
was falling hellward and wanted neither wind nor
tide to carry him, should now alter his course and
sail to a new port, this is a work indeed! It was by a
miracle that the river Jordan was driven back. To see
the earthly man become heavenly, to see a sinner
move contrary to himself in the ways of Christ and
holiness, is as strange as to see the earth fly upward
or the ball run contrary to its own path.

Salvation work is difficult with regard to the deceits about the work. The heart is ready to take many
false stitches in this work of salvation. It has the
heart of self-deceit. Therefore Augustine cried out,
"The heart is a great deep." The heart is apt to be
deceived about this work of salvation in two ways.

It will often make a man take morality for grace.
Alas, morality is but nature refined, old Adam put in
a better dress. A moralized man is but a tame devil!
There may be a fair stream of civility running and
yet much vermin of pride and atheism lying at the
bottom. The garnishment of moral excellencies is
but setting a garland of flowers upon a dead man.
How easy is it to be deceived in the business of salvation and, with Ixion, to embrace a cloud instead of
Juno! Civility is not grace, though it is a good wall to

plant the vine of grace against.

The heart will also be ready to deceive us in this work of salvation by making us take a show of grace for grace. Pliny said that there is a beryl stone that resembles the true diamond. So there is something that looks like grace but is not. There are two graces which help much to the working out of salvation, but we are soon deceived by their counterfeits.

The first grace is repentance. True repentance is when we weep for sin as sin, when we weep for it because it is a defiling thing. It blots the image of God and stains the virginity of the soul. It is an act of unkindness; it is a kicking against the breast that gives us milk. But how easy is it to prevaricate in this!

Many think they repent when it is not the offense, but the penalty that troubles them; not the treason, but the bloody axe.

They think they repent when they shed a few tears, but though this ice begins to melt a little, it freezes again and they still go on in sin. Many weep for their unkind dealings with God, as Saul did for his unkindness to David. "He said to David, 'Thou art more righteous than I for thou hast rewarded me good, whereas I have rewarded thee evil' " (1 Samuel 24:17). So men can lift up their voice and weep for sin, yet follow their sins again. They are like a snake that casts off its coat, but keeps its sting. There is as much difference between false and true tears as between channel water and spring water.

Another grace conducible to salvation is faith; but how easily are men deceived with a counterfeit pearl! There is this deceit about faith: men apply the promises of the Word, but not the precepts.

The promise is salvation; the precept is "working out." They will take the one but not the other, as if a physician should prescribe two medicines to his patient, a pill and a julep. He will take the julep because it is pleasant, but not the pill. Many will take Christ as a Savior, but refuse Him as a Prince; receive His benefits, but not submit to His laws. This is to put asunder what God has joined together. There being, therefore, such mistakes and deceits about this work of salvation, we need to be all the more cautious and curious in this work.

Third, the difficulty about salvation work arises from the hindrances of this work. These hindrances are from within, that is, the flesh. This is a sly enemy. The flesh cries out for ease; "it lusts against the Spirit" (Galatians 5:17). We are bid to crucify the flesh (Galatians 5:24), but how many wounds must we give with the sword of the Spirit before the flesh will be perfectly crucified?

We meet with hindrances in this work from without, from temptations. Augustine said our whole life is a temptation. We tread among snares. There is a snare in recreation, yes, our table is often a snare. Satan is still fishing for our souls. How often does he lay a train of temptation to blow up our fort of grace? The Apostle tells us of his fiery darts (Ephesians 6:16). Temptations are called darts for their swiftness—they are shot in swiftly—and fiery for their terribleness. They are shot like flashes of fire into the soul which amaze and frighten, and does not this retard the work of salvation and make it difficult?

We meet with hindrances in this work from reproaches. Acts 28:22: "This sect is everywhere spoken against." The old serpent is ever spitting his venom at religion and the professors of it. I may allude to 1 Corinthians 10:1: "All our fathers were under a cloud." All the saints of old have passed to heaven under a cloud of rude language and reproach. The world puts them in their black book whom God will put in His book in red letters! The throat of the wicked is an open sepulchre to bury the good names of those who have been the ensign-bearers of religion and have carried her colors.

Sometimes they have been defamed and slandered. Paul was reported to be a seditious man (2 Timothy 2:9). The popish Rhemists defamed Calvin and blamed him for teaching that God was the author of sin and they said that Calvin died cursing, though Beza, who was an eyewitness and wrote his life and death, confuted that slander and related what a comfortable end he had. As for Martin Bucer, that blessed man who cried out in a holy triumph, "I am Christ's and the devil has nothing to do with me," yet the papists slanderously report that he denied that Christ was the Messiah come in the flesh. But he who was the orator at his funeral vouched for his character under oath.

The Jesuits in Burgundia commit the same slander of Beza, that holy man. They say that he, perceiving death to be at hand, renounced his former profession of the gospel and was perfectly reconciled to the church at Rome. This was so false that Beza, who lived after the slander went abroad, himself refuted it with great indignation.

Sometimes the saints have had the trial of cruel

mockings (Hebrews 11:36). Cyprian was called, in a jeer, Coprian; Athanasius, Satanus; David was the song of the drunkards (Psalm 69:12). I do not doubt but that Noah had many a bitter taunt when he was building the ark so many years before the flood. They would laugh at him and censure him as an old, doting fool who would be wiser than all the world besides. Thus when we see the flood of God's wrath coming upon the world and we begin to build the ark and "work out salvation," men will be venting their scorn and derision: "What? You will be holier than others? More precise than necessary?" All this serves to retard salvation work and make it difficult.

A third hindrance in this work is open violence. Galatians 4:29: "As he that was born after the flesh persecuted him that was born after the Spirit, so it is now." No sooner does a man give up his name to Christ and seriously set upon the working out of his salvation, but the world raises her trained bands and sets all the militia of hell against him. God's church is like Abraham's ram tied in a bush of thorns. Witness the ten persecutions in the time of Nero, Domitian, and Trajan. A man who is strictly holy is the target that is shot at. If the world's music will not prevail, it has its furnace ready (2 Timothy 3:12). Be assured that Christ and His cross are never parted. It is with us in our building for heaven as it was with the Jews in their building the wall: "everyone with one of his hands wrought the work, and with the other hand held a weapon" (Nehemiah 4:17). So we must not only be builders, but warriors. With one hand we must work, and with the other hand hold a weapon, namely the sword of the Spirit, and fight the good fight of faith. This is yet another hindrance in the work. No sooner do we begin to set out for heaven, but "bonds and afflictions abide us" (Acts 20:23). The world sounds an alarm and there will be no cessation of arms until death.

That which makes salvation work hard is that it is a slippery work. "Look to yourselves that we lose not those things which we have wrought" (2 John 8). This work falls down almost as fast as we build. An ordinary craftsman, when he has been at work, finds his work the next morning just as he left it, but it is not so with us. When we have been working out salvation by prayer, fasting, and meditation, and we leave this work awhile, we shall not find our work as we left it. A great deal of our work will have fallen down again.

We need to be called upon often "to strengthen the things which are ready to die" (Revelation 3:2). No sooner is a Christian taken off from the fire of the sanctuary, but he is ready to cool and freeze again in security. He is like a watch: when he has been wound up towards heaven, he quickly unwinds to earth and sin again. When the gold has been purified in the furnace, it remains pure, but it is not so with the heart. Let it be heated in an ordinance, let it be purged in the fire of affliction. It does not remain pure, but quickly gathers oil and corruption. We are seldom long in a good frame. All this shows how difficult the work of salvation is. We must not only work, but set a watch, too!

QUESTION 1. But why has God made the way to heaven so hard? Why must there be this working?

ANSWER 1. To make us set a high estimate upon

heavenly things. If salvation were easily come by, we should not have valued its worth. If diamonds were ordinary they would be slighted, but because they are hard to come by they are in great esteem. Tertullian said that when pearls grew common in Rome, people wore them on their shoes, which was the next way to tread them under their feet. Salvation is such a pearl as God will not have slighted. Therefore, it must be acquired by holy industry. God will not allow the price of spiritual mercies to fall. Those who would have this precious flower of salvation must gather it in the sweat of their brows.

We must work and take pains that we may be fitted for heaven. A father will give his son the inheritance, but first he will give him an education that he may be fit for it. God will settle salvation upon us, but first He "makes us meet for the inheritance" (Colossians 1:12). While we are working, we are running and fitting for heaven. Sin is weakening, grace is ripening. While we are in combat, we are fitting for the crown. First you season the vessel before you pour in the wine. God will season us with grace before He pours in the wine of glory.

QUESTION 2. But if there must be this working, how is it said that Christ's yoke is easy?

ANSWER 2. To the fleshly part, it is hard, but where there is a new and holy principle infused, Christ's yoke is easy. It is not a yoke, but a crown. When the wheels of the soul are oiled with grace, then a Christian moves in the way of religion with facility and alacrity. A child delights in obeying his father. It was Paul's heaven to serve God. "I delight

in the law of God in the inner man" (Romans 7:22).
And how swiftly is the soul carried upon those
wings! Christ's service is Christ's freedom, therefore
the Apostle calls it "a law of liberty" (James 1:25).

To serve God, to love God, to enjoy God is the
sweetest liberty in the world. Christ does not, as did
Pharaoh, "make his people serve with rigor" (Exodus 1:13), but He lays upon them the "constraints of
love" (2 Corinthians 5:14). His precepts are not burdens, but privileges; not fetters, but ornaments.
Thus His yoke is easy, but to an unregenerate man
the yoke has a nail in it. It galls and vexes. As far as
corruption prevails, the best heart finds some reluc-
tance. And so much for the first reason, the difficulty of the work.

REASON 2. *The second reason why we must put forth so
much holy sweat and industry about salvation is because of
the rareness of this work.* Few shall be saved; therefore
we need to work all the harder that we may be in the
number of those few. The way to hell is a broad way
paved with riches and pleasure. It has a golden pave-
ment, and therefore there are so many travellers on
it, but the way to heaven lies out of the road. It is an
unbeaten path, and few can find it.

The criers of universal grace say that Christ died
intentionally for all, but then why are not all saved?
Can Christ be frustrated of His intention? Some are
so gross as to aver that all shall actually be saved, but
has our Lord Christ not told us, "the gate is strait,
and few there be that find it" (Matthew 7:14)? How
all can go in at this gate and yet but a few find it
seems to me to be a paradox. The drove of men goes

to shambles, "but a remnant shall be saved" (Romans 9:27). The whole piece is cut off and goes to the devil. Only a remnant shall be saved. Most of the people in the world are windfalls. That olive tree in Isaiah 17:6 with two or three olive berries on the top of the uppermost bough may be a fit emblem of the scarcity of those that shall be saved. Satan goes away with the harvest. God has only a few gleanings. In this great city, if it should go by vote and by poll, the devil would carry it.

Some of the learned observe that if you were to divide the world into thirty equal parts, nineteen of those thirty are overrun with heathenish idolatry, six of the remaining eleven with the doctrine of Mohammed, so that there remain but five parts of the thirty where there is anything of Christianity. Among those "Christians" are so many seduced papists on the one hand and formal Protestants on the other that surely there are few that are saved. It being thus, it should make us strive all the more that we may be of the number of those few who shall inherit salvation.

REASON 3. *The third reason why we should put forth so much vigor about the work of salvation is because of the possibility of the work.* Impossibility kills all endeavor. Who will take pains for that which he thinks there is no hope of ever obtaining? But "there is hope in Israel concerning this" (Ezra 10:2). Salvation is a thing that is feasible; it may be had. O Christians, though the gate of paradise is narrow, yet the gate is open. It is shut against the devils, but is open to you. Who would not crowd hard to get in? It is but paring off your sins, it is but unloading some of your thick clay, it is but abating the swelling humor of your pride, and you may get in at the narrow gate. This possibility, nay probability, of salvation may put your life into your endeavor. If there is corn to be had, why should you sit starving in your sins any longer?

USE 1. OF INFORMATION.

It shows that salvation is not as facile a thing as most imagine. Many fancy a fine, easy way to heaven; a sigh, or tear, or "Lord, have mercy" will save them. Those who believe this are in a golden dream. The text tells us of working out salvation. Basil compares the way to heaven to a man going over a narrow bridge. If he treads ever so much aside, he falls in and drowns. He that thinks the way is easy is never yet in the way. There are so many precepts to obey, so many promises to believe, so many temptations to resist that we shall not find the easy way.

There must not only be diligence, but violence. Beloved, heaven's gate is not like that iron gate which opened to Peter of its own accord in Acts 12:10. No, there must be knocking and striving. Jacob obtained the blessing in the garments of Esau. The name "Esau" in Hebrew signifies "working." If you would wear this embroidered garment of salvation, you must have it by way of working: "work out your own salvation." Hannibal forged a way for his army over the Alps. We must forge our way to glory through difficulties. I like the example one man gave of a hand with a pick axe digging a way through a rock with this motto: "I WILL EITHER FIND A WAY OR MAKE ONE!"

We must go to heaven through sweat and blood. There is nothing gotten without hard labor. You cannot have the world without labor, and would you have Christ and salvation without it? Do men dig for lead and not much more for gold? It is observable that Adam in paradise was not idle, but he dressed the vineyard. The angels themselves, though they are glorious spirits, are yet ministering spirits (Hebrews 1:14). God has put this diligence into creatures void of reason. The bee is a most industrious creature; all of them have their own work to do in the hive. Some of the bees trim the honey, some work the wax, some frame the comb, and others lie as sentinels at the door of the hive to keep out the drone. Is the bee so industrious by the instinct of nature in the working of honey? Oh, how industrious ought we to be in the working out of salvation!

USE 2. OF REPROOF.

Out of this text, as a spiritual quiver, I may draw several arrows of reproof.

1. It reproves those who prefer other things before salvation, who labor more for the bread that perishes than for salvation. Their chief care is how to live in the world and get a present subsistence. "All the labor of a man is for his mouth" (Ecclesiastes 6:7). The body shall be tended to and looked after, which is but the brutish part, but the poor soul is kept to hard rations. This will cause Christians to turn into heathens. Matthew 6:32: "For after these things the Gentiles seek." God never sent us here only to wear fine clothes or fare sumptuously every day, but that we should drive a trade for salvation. If

this is not done, we have shot beside the mark all this while. We have but trimmed the scabbard and let the soul, that blade of admirable mettle, rust and canker.

2. It reproves such as, instead of working, stand idle all the day in the vineyard. They wish for salvation, but do not work. The idle Christian is like a soldier who has a good mind to the spoil and treasure of a castle but is loath to put himself to any trouble or hazard. Men could be content to have salvation if it would, like the ripe figs of Nahum 3:12, "fall into the mouth of the eater." The sluggard "puts his hand into his bosom" (Proverbs 19:24), and is loath to pluck it out, though it is to lay hold of a crown. "They stretch themselves upon the beds of ivory" (Amos 6:4). Men would rather lie upon a soft bed than go to heaven in a fiery chariot of zeal.

Chrysostom calls idleness the root of despair. An idle Christian doles out his time unprofitably. He stands in the world for a cipher, and be assured that God writes down no ciphers in the Book of Life. An idle person is a fit subject for the devil to work upon. We do not sow seed in fallow ground, but the devil sows most of his seed of temptation in hearts that lie fallow. Jerome makes this observation about the crabfish. While the oyster opens itself, the crabfish flings a little stone into its mouth so that the oyster cannot shut itself and so the crab devours it. The devil is like this crab when he takes men gaping (as is usual for those who are idle); then he throws in his stones of temptation and so devours them.

3. It reproves those who, instead of making religion a work, make it a play. These are they who have

found a new way to heaven, who make the way easier than ever did Christ! Such as tell us that there is no law to a believer, and if there is no law then there is no transgression, and if there is no transgression, then no repentance is needed. Between the Arminian and the antinomian, it is a very short cut to heaven. The Arminian says we have power in ourselves to believe, and the antinomian says that a believer is not under any Law; he is bound to no duty. Christ has done all for him, so that by taking this stride he is presently in heaven. If this doctrine is true, then every day is a play day and the Apostle made a mistake when he said, "work out your salvation."

4. It reproves those who, instead of working out their salvation, dispute away their salvation; such as would dispute against the authority of Scripture and would make our faith a fable; such as dispute against the immortality of the soul and so at once would pull down the court of conscience; such as dispute against the divinity of Christ. This may be called, indeed, the doctrine of devils (1 Timothy 4:1). It is a doctrine diametrically opposed to that Scripture in 1 John 5:20: "We are in Him that is true, even in His Son, Jesus Christ; this is the true God." This text is a bulwark against the Socinian.

Oh, the patience of God that for those who open their mouths blasphemously against Christ the earth does not open her mouth and swallow them up! That such should have any connivance who dare impugn the divinity of the Son of God is a lamentation, and shall be for a lamentation. Some of the best heathen writers (Livy, Aristotle, Plutarch) af-

firm that there were edicts and punishments enacted by heathen princes and states in matters of religion. A heathen would not suffer his god to be
blasphemed, and shall Christians suffer it?

5. It reproves those who, instead of pursuing
their own salvation, pursue their own destruction.
These are profane persons who go to hell in the
sweat of their own brows.

Drunkards. What they get in the temple, they lose
in the tavern. They steep the sermons they hear in
wine. "Woe to the drunkards in Ephraim" (Isaiah
28:1). I may change the word and say "the drunkards
of England." There is a kind of wine you call lach-
ryme, which signifies "tears." Such a wine the
damned drink, which is burned with the wrath of
God, and this shall be the drunkard's cup.

Swearers. They swear away their salvation. The
swearer, it seems, has bad credit. He must stake
down an oath or none will trust him. But let him
remember he runs his soul into a warning: "Swear
not at all" (Matthew 5:34). If we must give an account
for idle words, shall not idle oaths be put in the account book? When the scab breaks forth in the lip,
that man is to be pronounced unclean. Every oath is
a wound given to the soul, and every wound has a
mouth to cry to heaven for vengeance. Some are
boiled up to that height of wickedness that, like
mad dogs, they fly in the face of heaven by cursing.
And let a minister tell them of their sin, let him but
go about to bring them home again, as the law provided that one should bring home his neighbor's
ass when he went astray (Exodus 23:4), and they will
kick against the reproof. As with lime, pouring on

the water of a reprehension only makes them more
inflamed. These are upon the spur to damnation,
but I will not tred this path any longer.

Adulterers. The adulterer's heart, like the swearer's tongue, is set on fire by hell. Creatures void of
reason will rise up in judgment against such. It is
reported of the stork, that chaste creature, that it
confines itself to its own nest, and if any of the
storks leaves his own mate and joins with any other,
the rest fall upon him and pluck his feathers from
him. God would have the adulterer put to death
(Deuteronomy 22:22). Gregory observes, concerning
the stream of fire and brimstone poured upon
Sodom, that God sent that noisome plague to let
them see the filthiness of their sin. This sin of adul-
tery is a soul-damning sin (1 Corinthians 6:9). The
adulterer, like the fly, flies so long around the candle that at last he singes his soul. This sin, though it
began comically, it ends tragically! Will it not be
"bitterness in the end" (2 Samuel 2:26)? This sweet
calm is before an earthquake. After the woman's
hair come the lion's teeth.

6. It reproves those who put off this great work of
salvation until they are past their labor. They put off
repenting until old age and sickness.

Until old age. When they are fit for no other work,
then they will begin this. Old age is no good age to
repent in. When the fingers are stiff, it is hard learning to play the lute. When the heart is grown hard
and stiff in wickedness, it is hard to tune the peni-
tential string. A tender plant is easily removed, but it
is hard to pluck up an old tree that is rooted. An old
sinner who has been a long time rooting in sin is

hardly plucked out of his natural estate. In matters
of salvation, it is dangerous to adjourn. The longer
men go on in sin, the more full possession Satan
has of them. The longer poison stays in the stomach, the more deadly it is.

It is madness to put off the work of salvation until evening and sunset. "The night cometh when no
man can work" (John 9:4). It would be a very unwise
course for a mariner, while the ship is sound, the
tackling strong, the wind favorable, and the sea
calm, to lie idle at anchor, and when the ship begins to leak and the tempest to rise, then to launch
forth and hoist up sails for a voyage. So is he who
neglects the time of health and strength and, when
old age comes and his tackling is even broken, then
begins his voyage toward heaven.

It is very questionable whether God will accept repentance when it is so late. He calls for the first
fruits, and do we think to put Him off with the
gleanings? This was not the least reason why God re-
jected Cain's offering, because it was so long before
he brought it. "In process of time, Cain brought the
fruit of the ground" (Genesis 4:3), or, as the original
is more emphatic, "at the end of many days." It
seems it was stale before he brought it. How unwor-
thy is this, for men to give the devil their strength
and marrow and then to come and lay their old
bones before God's altar! It is true God may show
mercy at last, but such run a desperate hazard. A
sinner, in the time of his old age, sleeps between
death and the devil as Peter slept between two soldiers.

Until sickness. He would be very unwise who,

preparing to go on a long journey, should lay the
heaviest load on the weakest horse. What impru-
dence is it to lay the heavy load of repentance on
yourself when you have been made feeble by sickness! When the hands shake, the lips quiver, the
sinews shrink, the heart faints? Perhaps you shall
have no time of sickness, perhaps you will not have
the use of your senses. Perhaps God will deny you
His grace, and then where is your repentance? It is
just that he who forgets God in the time of health,
God should forget him in the time of sickness.

7. It reproves those who begin to work, but do not
work out their salvation. It is not enough to begin
well. Some have, like Jehu, driven furiously in religion, but within awhile their chariot wheels have
fallen off. We live in the fall of the leaf. We have observed several who once put forth fair blossoms and
gave good hopes of conversion, but their spring is
turned into autumn. They have stopped working for
heaven, a sign that the motion was only artificial,
not vital. "Israel hath cast off the thing that is good"
(Hosea 8:3). Such as were once diligent and zealous
in prayer, hearing, and holy conference, now have
left off the thing that is good. They have tired in
their march to heaven.

I have often thought that there are many who
may be compared to Nebuchadnezzar's image in
Daniel 3. At first they seemed to have a head of gold.
They looked like glorious professors. Then afterwards they seemed to be silver, then brass, then iron,
then clay. They have at last degenerated into sin.
Thus, like fair mornings, they have soon become
overcast. Epiphanius tells of the Gnostics that at

first they seemed to be a strict, holy people, but afterwards fell to libertinism. Some have grown so impudent that they brag of their apostasy. Time was when they read and prayed in their families, but now they thank God that they have grown wiser and they cease from these duties. It is just as if you should hear the devil boast that once he was an angel of light, but now he is turned into an angel of darkness. Apostates are the richest spoils that Satan goes away with. He will hang these up in hell for triumph. Such as have left off working, let them read that thundering Scripture in 2 Peter 2:21, "For it had been better for them not to have known the way of righteousness, than after they have known it to turn from the holy commandment." By leaving off working, they unravel all that they have done before. They lose their reward. He that runs half the race and then faints loses the garland.

USE 3. OF EXHORTATION.

And so I proceed to the next use to persuade you all in the bowels of Christ to set upon this great work, the working out of your salvation. Beloved, here is a plot for heaven, and I would have you all in this plot. Rally together all the powers of your souls. Give neither God nor yourselves rest until you have made your election sure. Christians, fall to work. Do it early, earnestly, incessantly. Pursue salvation as in a holy chase. Other things are but matters of convenience; salvation is a matter of necessity. Either you must do the work that Christians are doing or you must do the work that devils are doing. Oh, you who never yet took one stitch in this work of salvation, begin now. Religion is a good trade if it is well followed. Be assured that there is no salvation without working, but here I must lay down a caution to prevent mistakes.

CAUTION. Though we are not saved *without* working, yet we are not saved *for* our working. Bellarmine said we merit heaven out of unworthiness. No, though we are saved in the use of means, yet this is by grace too (Ephesians 2:5). There must be plowing and sowing the ground, but no crops can be expected without the influence of the sun. So there must be working, but no crop of salvation can be hoped for without the sunshine of free grace. "'Tis your Father's good pleasure to give you the kingdom" (Luke 12:32). Give? "Why," some might say, "we have worked hard for it!" Aye, but heaven is a donation. Though you work for it, yet it is the good pleasure of God to bestow it. Still look up to Christ's merit. It is not your sweat but His blood that saves.

It is clear that your working cannot merit salvation. Philippians 2:13: "'Tis God that works in you to will and to do." It is not your working, but God's coworking. For as the scrivener guides the child's hand or he cannot write, so the Spirit of God must afford His auxiliary concurrence or our work stands still. How, then, can any man merit by working when it is God who helps him to work?

I should now, having laid down this caution, resume the exhortation and persuade you to the working out of salvation; but I must first remove two objections which lie in the way:

OBJECTION 1. You bid us to work out salvation, but we have no power to work.

ANSWER. It is true, we have no power. I deny that we have free will. Man before conversion is purely passive. Therefore Ezekiel 36:26 calls it "a heart of stone." A man in his pure, natural state can no more prepare himself to his own converting than the stone can prepare itself to its own softening. But yet, when God begins to draw, we may follow. Those dry bones in Ezekiel could not, of themselves, live, but when breath came into them, then "they lived and stood upon their feet" (Ezekiel 37:10).

QUESTION. But suppose God has not dropped in a principle of grace? Suppose He has not caused breath to enter?

ANSWER. Yet use the means. Though you cannot work spiritually, yet work physically. Do what you are able to do, and that for two reasons.

1. Because a man, by neglecting the means, destroys himself just as a man, by not sending for the physician, may be said to be the cause of his own death.

2. God is not wanting to us when we do what we are able. Urge the promise, "Seek and ye shall find" (Matthew 7:7). Put this promise to work by prayer. You say you have no power, but have you not a promise? Act as far as you can. Though I dare not say, as the Arminian, that when we exert and put forth nature God is bound to give grace, yet I do say God is not wanting to those who seek His grace. Nay, I will say more. He denies His grace to none but them that willfully refuse it.

OBJECTION 2. But to what purpose should I

work? There is a decree passed. If God has decreed I
shall be saved, I shall be saved.

ANSWER. God decrees salvation in a way of working (2 Thessalonians 2:13). Origen, in his book
against Celsus, observes a subtle argument of some
who disputed about fate and destiny. One gave
counsel to his sick friend not to send for the physician because, he said, it is appointed by destiny
whether you shall recover or not. If it is your destiny
to recover, then you do not need the physician, and
if it is not your destiny, then the physician will do
you no good.

The same fallacy is used by the devil against men.
He bids them not to work. If God has decreed that
they shall be saved, they shall be saved and there is
no need of working. If He has not decreed their salvation, then their working will do them no good.
This is an argument fetched out of the devil's rea-
soning. But we say that God decrees the end in the
use of the means. God decreed that Israel should enter into Canaan, but first they had to fight with the
sons of Anak. God decreed that Hezekiah should recover out of his sickness, but let him lay a fig to the
boil (Isaiah 38:21).

We do not argue this way in other things. A man
does not say, "If God has decreed that I shall have a
crop this year, I shall have a crop! What need do I
have to plow, or sow, or fertilize the land?" No, he
will use the means and expect a crop. Though "the
blessing of the Lord makes rich" (Proverbs 10:22),
yet it is just as true that "the diligent hand makes
rich" (Proverbs 10:4). God's decreeing is carried on
by our working.

And thus, having removed these objections out of the way, let me now persuade you to set upon this blessed work, the working out of your salvation. And, that my words might better prevail, I shall propound several arguments by way of motive to excite you to this work.

1. The first argument or motive to working is taken from the preciousness of the soul. Well may we take pains that we may secure this from danger. The soul is a divine spark kindled by the breath of God. It outweighs the world (Matthew 16:26). If the world is the book of God, as Origen calls it, the soul is the image of God. Plato calls the soul a glass of the Trinity. It is a bright mirror in which some refracted beams of God's wisdom and holiness shine forth. The soul is a blossom of eternity.

God has made the soul capable of communion with Himself. It would bankrupt the world to give half the price of a soul. How highly did Christ value the soul when He sold Himself to buy it! Oh, then, what a pity is it that this excellent soul, this soul for which God called a council in heaven when He made it, should miscarry and be undone to all eternity! Who would not rather work night and day than lose such a soul? The jewel is invaluable, the loss irreparable.

2. Holy activity and industry ennoble a Christian. The more excellent anything is, the more active it is. The sun is a glorious creature. It never stands still but is always going on its circuit around the world. Fire is the purest element and the most active; it is ever sparkling and flaming. The angels are the most noble creatures and the most nimble. Therefore,

they are represented by cherubim with their wings displayed. God Himself is a most pure act.

Homer said of Agamemnon that he sometimes resembled Jupiter in feature, Pallas in wisdom, Mars in valor. By holy activity we resemble God who is a most pure act. The phoenix flies with a coronet on its head. The industrious Christian does not need a coronet; his sweat ennobles him. His labor is his ensign of honor. Solomon tells us that "drowsiness clothes a man with rags" (Proverbs 23:21). Infamy is one of the rags that hang upon him. God hates a dull temper. We read in the Law that the ass, being a dull creature, must not be offered up in sacrifice. Spiritual activity is a badge of honor.

3. Working out salvation is that which will make death and heaven sweet to us.

It will sweeten death. He who has been hard at work all day, how quietly does he sleep at night! You who have been working out your salvation all your lives, how comfortably may you lay down your head at night in the grave upon a pillow of dust in hope of a glorious resurrection! This will be a deathbed comfort.

It will sweeten heaven. The more pains we have taken for heaven, the sweeter it will be when we come there. It is delightful for a man to look over his work and see the fruit appear. When he has been planting trees in his orchard or setting flowers, it is pleasant to behold and review his labors. Thus in heaven, when we shall see the fruit of our labors, "the end of our salvation" (1 Peter 1:9), this will make heaven the sweeter. The more pains we have taken for heaven, the more welcome it will be. The more sweat, the more sweet. When a man has been sinning, the pleasure is gone and the sting remains, but when he has been repenting, the labor is gone and the joy remains.

You still have time to work. This text and sermon would be out of season to preach to the damned in hell. If I should bid them work, it is too late. Their time is past. It is night with the devil, it is still day with you. "Work while it is day" (John 9:4). If you lose your day, you lose your souls. This is the season for your souls. Now God commands, now the Spirit breathes, now ministers beseech, and as so many bells of Aaron would chime in your souls to Christ, oh, improve the season. This is your seed time; now sow the seeds of faith and repentance. If when you have seasons you lack hearts, the time may come when you have hearts and shall lack seasons. Take time while you may. The mariner hoists up his sails while the wind blows.

Never did a people have a fairer gale for heaven than you of this city do, and will you not set forward in your voyage? What riding is there to the term? I assure you the Lawyer will not lose His term. Oh, my brethren, now is the time for your souls. Plead with God for mercy, or at least get Christ to plead for you.

Think seriously on these eight things:

1. Our life unravels swiftly. Gregory compares our life to the mariner in a ship going full sail. We are every day sailing swiftly to eternity.

2. The seasons of grace, though they are precious, yet they are not permanent. Abused mercies will, like Noah's dove, take their wings and fly from us. England's golden hour will soon run out. Gospel

blessings are very sweet but very swift. "Now they are hid from thine eyes" (Luke 19:42). We know not how soon the golden candlesticks may be removed.

3. There is a time when the Spirit has finished striving. There are certain tides of the Spirit, and, these being neglected, it is possible that we may never see another tide come in. When conscience has finished speaking, usually the Spirit has stopped striving.

4. The loss of gospel opportunities will be the hell of hell. When a sinner shall think with himself at the last day, "Oh, what I might have been! I might have been as rich as the angels, as rich as heaven could make me. I had a season to work in, but I lost it," this will be as a vulture gnawing upon him. This will enhance and accent his misery, and let all this persuade you speedily to work out your salvation.

5. You may do this work and not hinder your other work. Working out salvation and working in a calling are not inconsistent. And this I insert to prevent an objection. Some may say, "But I work so hard for heaven that I shall have no time for my trade." Be sure that the wise God would never make any of His commands to conflict. As He would have you seek His kingdom (Matthew 6:33), so He would have you provide for your family (1 Timothy 5:8). You may drive two trades together. I do not like those who make the church exclude the shop, who swallow up all their time in hearing but neglect their work at home (2 Thessalonians 3:11). They are like the lilies of the field "which toil not, neither do they spin" (Matthew 6:28). God never sealed any warrant to idleness. He both commands and commends diligence

in a calling, which may rather encourage us to look
after salvation, because this work will not take us off
our other work. A man may follow God fully with
Caleb (Numbers 14:24), and yet, with David, "follow
the ewes great with young" (Psalm 78:71). Piety and
industry may dwell together.

6. Think on the inexcusableness of those who
neglect working out their salvation. I think I hear
God expostulating the case with men at the last day
after this manner: "Why did you not work? I gave you
time to work. I gave you light to work by. I gave you
My gospel, My Spirit, My ministers. I bestowed tal-
ents on you to trade. I set the recompense of reward
before you. Why did you not work out your salvation?
Either it must be sloth or stubbornness. Was there
any work you did of greater concern? You could
work in brick, but not in gold. What can you say for
yourselves as to why the sentence should not be
passed." Oh, how will the sinner be left speechless at
such a time, and how will this cut him to the heart
to think how he neglected salvation and could give
no reason for it.

7. Think on the inexpressible misery of those
who do not work out salvation. Those who sleep in
spring shall beg in harvest. After death, when they
look to receive a full crop of glory, they will be put to
beg for one drop of water as did Dives. Vagrant persons who will not work are sent to the house of cor-
rections. Such as will not work out salvation, let
them know that hell is God's house of correction
that they must be sent to.

8. If all this does not prevail, consider lastly what
it is we are working for. None will take pains for a

trifle. We are working for a crown, for a throne, for a paradise, and all this is comprised in that one word "salvation." Here is a whetstone to industry. All men desire salvation. It is the crown of our hopes. We should not think any labor too much for this. What pains will men take for earthly crowns and scepters! And suppose the kingdoms of the world were more illustrious than they are, their foundations of gold, their walls of pearl, their windows of sapphire. What is all this to that kingdom we are laboring for? We may as well span the firmament as set forth this in all its splendor and magnificence.

Salvation is a beautiful thing. It is as far above our thoughts as it is above our deserts. Oh, how should this add wings to our endeavors! The merchant will run through the intemperate zones of heat and cold for a little prize. The soldier, for a rich booty, will endure the bullet and the sword. He will gladly undergo a bloody spring for a golden harvest. Oh, then, how much more should we spend our holy sweat for this blessed prize of salvation!

DIRECTIONS. And so, having laid down some arguments by way of motive to persuade us to this work, I shall now propound some means by way of direction to help us in this work. And here I shall show you what are those things to be removed which will hinder our working, and what are those things to be followed which will further it.

We must remove those things which will hinder our working out salvation. There are six bars in the way to salvation which must be removed.

1. The entanglements of the world. While the

foot is in a snare, a man cannot run. The world is a
snare. While our feet are in it, we cannot "run the
race that is set before us" (Hebrews 12:1). If a man
were to climb up a steep rock with weights tied to
his legs, they would hinder his ascent. Too many
golden weights will hinder us from climbing up this
steep rock that leads to salvation. While the mill of a
trade is going, it makes such a noise that we can
hardly hear the minister lifting up his voice like a
trumpet. The world chokes our zeal and appetite for
heavenly things. The earth puts out our fire, the music of the world charms us to sleep, and then we
cannot work. In gold mines there are deadly gases.
Oh, how many souls have been destroyed with a gas
arising from the earth!

2. The second bar in the way to salvation is sadness and uncheerfulness. When a man's heart is
sad, he is unfit to go about his work; he is like an
untuned instrument. Under fears and discourage-
ments we act but faintly in religion. David labors to
chide himself out of this spiritual melancholy: "Why
art thou cast down, O my soul?" (Psalm 42:5). Cheerfulness quickens. The Lacedaemonians used music
in their battles to excite their spirits and make them
fight more valiantly. Cheerfulness is like music to
the soul; it excites to duty. It oils the wheels of the affections. Cheerfulness makes service come off with
delight, and we are never carried so swiftly in religion as upon the wings of delight. Melancholy takes
off our chariot wheels, and then we drive on heavily.

3. The third bar to salvation is spiritual sloth.
This is a great impediment to our working. It was
said of Israel, "they despised the pleasant land"

(Psalm 106:24). What should be the reason? Canaan was a paradise of delight, a type of heaven. Aye, but they thought it would cost them a great deal of trouble and hazard to get it, and they would rather go without it. They despised the pleasant land. Are there not millions among us who would rather go sleeping to hell than sweating to heaven? I have read of certain Spaniards who live near where there is a great store of fish, yet they are so lazy that they will not take the pains to catch them. They buy them off of their neighbors! Such a sinful stupidity and sloth are upon most so that, though Christ is near them, though salvation is offered in the gospel, yet they will not work out salvation. "Slothfulness casts into a deep sleep" (Proverbs 19:15). Adam lost his rib when he was asleep, and many a man loses his soul in this deep sleep.

4. The fourth bar in the way to salvation is an opinion of the easiness of salvation: "God is merciful, and, if worst comes to worst, we need only to repent."

God is merciful, it is true, but with all He is just. He must not wrong His justice by showing mercy. Therefore, observe that clause in the proclamation, Exodus 34:7, "He will by no means clear the guilty." If a king proclaimed that only those should be pardoned who came in and submitted to his scepter, could any still persisting in rebellion claim the benefit of that pardon? Oh, sinner, would you have mercy, and will you not disband the weapons of unrighteousness?

"Only repent"? It is such an "only" that we cannot hit unless God directs our arrow. Tell me, O

sinner, is it easy for a dead man to live and walk?
You are spiritually dead and wrapped up in your
winding sheet (Ephesians 2:1). Is regeneration easy?
Are there no pangs in the new birth? Is self-denial
easy? Do you know what religion must cost, and
what it may cost? It must cost you parting with your
lusts, and it may cost you parting with your life! Take
heed of this obstruction. Salvation is not *per saltum.* It
is not a walk through the forest. Thousands have
gone to hell upon this mistake. The broad specta-
cles of presumption have made the narrow gate
seem wider than it is.

5. The fifth bar in the way to salvation is carnal
friends. It is dangerous to listen to their voice. The
serpent spoke in Eve. Job's wife would have called
him off from serving God, "Dost thou still retain
thine integrity?" (Job 2:9). What, still pray and weep?
Here the devil handed a temptation to Job through
his wife. Carnal friends will be calling us off from
our work: "What is the need for all this ado? Less
pains will serve."

We read that some of Christ's kindred, when they
saw Christ so earnest in His preaching, would have
checked Him. Mark 3:21: "His friends went to lay
hold on Him." Our friends and kindred would
sometimes stand in our path to heaven, and, judging our zeal as madness, would lay hold of us and
hinder us from working out our salvation. Such
friends Spira met with, seeking their advice as to
whether he should revoke his former opinion concerning Luther's doctrine or persist in it to his
death. They wished him to recant, and so, openly ad-
juring his former faith, he became like a living man

in hell.

6. The sixth bar in the way to salvation is evil company. They will take us off our work. Sweet waters lose their freshness when they run into salt water. Christians lose their freshness and savor among the wicked. Christ's doves will be sullied by "lying among these pots" (Psalm 68:13). Sinful company is like the water in a blacksmith's forge which quenches the iron, be it never so hot. Such people cool good affections. The wicked have the "plague of the heart" (1 Kings 8:38), and their breath is infectious. They will discourage us from working out our salvation.

If a man were a suitor to a woman and very earnest in his pursuit of her, and then one came to him with a bad report of her, with some impediment he would, upon hearing this, cease his pursuit of her. So it is with many a man who begins to be a suitor of religion. He would willingly have the match made up, and he grows very hot and violent in the suit and sets to working out his salvation, but then some of his confederates come and tell him that they know something bad about religion. "This sect is everywhere spoken against" (Acts 28:22). There must be so much strictness and mortification that he must never look to see a good day again. Hereupon he is discouraged and so the match is broken off. Take heed of such persons; they are devils covered with flesh. They are, as one has said, like Herod, who would have killed Christ as soon as He was born. Thus, when Christ is beginning to be formed in the heart, they would, in a spiritual sense, kill Him.

HELPS. And thus I have shown you the bars that
lie in the way to salvation which must be removed. I
now proceed, in the second place, to lay down some
helps conducive to salvation.

The first is in the text: "fear and trembling." This
is not a fear of doubting, but a fear of diligence.
This fear is requisite in the working out of salvation.
"Let us fear lest we come short" (Hebrews 4:1). Fear
is a remedy against presumption. Fear is that flaming sword that turns every way to keep sin from entering. Fear quickens, it is an antidote against sloth.
"Noah, being moved with fear, prepared an ark"
(Hebrews 11:7). The traveller, fearing lest night
should overtake him before he gets to his journey's
end, spurs on the faster.

Fear causes circumspection. He who walks in
fear treads warily. Fear is a preservative against apostasy, "I will put My fear in your hearts, and you shall
not depart from Me" (Jeremiah 32:40). The fear of
falling keeps us from falling. Fear is the badge and
livery of a Christian. The saints of old were men
fearing God (Malachi 3:16). It is reported of holy
Anselm that he spent most of his thoughts about
the day of judgment. "Blessed is he that fears always"
(Proverbs 28:14). Fear is a Christian's garrison; the
way to be secure is always to fear. This is one of the
best tools for a Christian to work with.

Second, another great help in working out salvation is love. Love makes the work come off with delight. Seven years' labor seemed as nothing to Jacob
because of the love that he bore for Rachel. Love fa-
cilitates everything. It is like wings to the bird, like
wheels to the chariot, like sails to the ship. It carries

on swiftly and cheerfully in duty. Love is never weary. It is an excellent saying of Gregory, "Let but a man get the love of the world in his heart, and he will quickly be rich." So if you will but get the love of religion in your heart, you will quickly be rich in grace. Love is a vigorous, active grace. It despises dangers, it tramples upon difficulties. Like a mighty torrent, it carries all before it. This is the grace which takes heaven by violence. Get but your hearts well heated with this grace and you will be fitted for work.

A third thing conducive to salvation is to work in the strength of Christ. "I can do all things through Christ that strengthens me" (Philippians 4:13). Never go to work alone. Samson's strength lay in his hair, and a Christian's strength lies in Christ. When you are to do any duty, to resist any temptation, to subdue any lust, set upon it in the strength of Christ. Some go out to fight sin in the strength of resolutions and vows. They are soon foiled. Do as Samson. He first cried to heaven for help, and then, having taken hold of the pillars, pulled down the house upon the lords of the Philistines. When we engage Christ in the work, and so take hold upon the pillar of an ordinance, we then bring down the house upon the head of our lusts.

Fourth, work low, be humble, do not think that you will merit anything by your working. Either Satan will keep us from working or else he will make us proud of our working. God must pardon our works before He crowns them. If we could pray as angels, shed rivers of tears, build churches, erect hospitals, and should have a conceit that we merited

anything by this, it would be as a dead fly in the box
of perfume. It would stain and eclipse the glory of
the work. Our duties, like good wine, taste of a bad
cask. They are but glittering sins. Let not pride poison our holy things. When we have been working
for heaven, we should say as did good Nehemiah,
"Remember me, O my God, concerning this, and
spare me according to the greatness of Thy mercy"
(Nehemiah 13:22).

Fifth, work upon your knees; be much in prayer.
Beg the Spirit of God to help you in the work. Make
that prayer, "Awake, O north wind, and come thou
south, blow upon my garden" (Song of Solomon
4:16). We need to have this Spirit blow upon us,
there being so many contrary winds blowing against
us, and considering how soon holy affections are
apt to wither. The garden does not need more wind
to make its fruit flow than we need of the Spirit to
make our graces flourish.

Philip joined himself to the eunuch's chariot.
God's Spirit must join itself to our chariot. As the
mariner has his hand to the stern, so he has his eyes
to the stars. While we are working, we must look up
to the Spirit. What is our preparation without the
Spirit's operation? What is all our rowing without a
gale from heaven? "The Spirit lifted me up" (Ezekiel
3:14). God's Spirit must both infuse grace and excite
it. We read of a wheel within a wheel (Ezekiel 1:16).
The Spirit of God is that inner wheel that must move
the wheel of our endeavors. To conclude all, pray to
God to bless you in your work. "The race is not to
the swift, nor the battle to the strong" (Ecclessiastes
9:11). Nothing prospers without a blessing, and

what way to obtain it but by prayer? It is a saying of one of the ancients, "The saints carry the keys of heaven at their girdle." Prayer beats the weapon out of the enemy's hands and gets the blessing out of God's hand.

Last, work in hope. The Apostle said, "He that plows shall plow in hope" (1 Corinthians 9:10). Hope is the soul's anchor (Hebrews 6:19). Cast this anchor upon the promise and you shall never sink. Nothing more hinders us in our working than unbelief. "Sure," said a Christian, "I may toil all the day and catch nothing." What? Is there no balm in Gilead? Is there no mercy seat? Oh, sprinkle faith in every duty; look up to free grace; fix your eye upon the blood of Christ! Would you be saved? To your working, join believing.